150 ESSENTIAL
WHOLE GRAIN
RECIPES

TRANSCONTINENTAL BOOKS
5800 Saint-Denis St.
Suite 900
Montreal, Que. H2S 3L5
Telephone: 514-273-1066
Toll-free: 1-800-565-5531
canadianliving.com

Bibliothèque et Archives nationales du
Québec and Library and Archives Canada
cataloguing in publication

Main entry under title:
150 essential whole grain recipes
Includes index.
ISBN 978-0-9877474-2-6
1. Cooking (Cereals). 2. Cereals as food.
3. Cookbooks. I. Canadian Living Test
Kitchen. II. Title: One hundred and fifty
essential whole grain recipes.

TX808.O54 2012   641.6'31
C2012-941187-6

Project editor: Christina Anson Mine
Copy editor: Jill Buchner
Indexer: Beth Zabloski
Art director and designer: Chris Bond

Printed in Canada
© Transcontinental Books, 2012
Legal deposit – 3rd quarter 2012
National Library of Quebec
National Library of Canada
ISBN 978-0-9877474-2-6

We acknowledge the financial support of
our publishing activity by the Government
of Canada through the Canada Book Fund.

For information on special rates for
corporate libraries and wholesale
purchases, please call 1-866-800-2500.

Turkey Pot Pie With
Cheese–Corn Bread Topping
(page 166)

Canadian Living

150 ESSENTIAL
WHOLE GRAIN
RECIPES

BY THE CANADIAN LIVING TEST KITCHEN

Transcontinental Books

EDITOR'S NOTE

EATING WHOLE GRAINS is definitely in vogue – and not just because whole, unrefined ingredients are healthy. Whole grains come in a variety of textures and flavours, and are far more interesting and complex than their refined counterparts. Why have steamed white rice when you can have flavourful, nutty brown rice pilau? Why not dig in to a crispy, delicious buckwheat waffle rather than settle for the plain old white-flour version?

For years, the prevailing attitude about whole grains and healthy eating was a little closed-minded. The truth is, you don't need to be the "crunchy granola" type to enjoy multigrain muesli, quinoa salad or barley risotto. Nor do you need to have a gluten intolerance in order to try (and love) the interesting gluten-free grains out there. And while wheat, oats, quinoa, barley, corn and brown rice are household staples, buckwheat, spelt, amaranth and millet are becoming more popular every day. In fact, these ingredients are widely available in supermarkets and bulk food stores across the country.

Whether you're a health nut or a regular joe, you'll find these recipes are tasty enough to satisfy. The fact that they're packed with vitamins, minerals and fibre? Well, that's just a delicious bonus.

Enjoy and eat well!

– Annabelle Waugh,
food director

CONTENTS

WHOLE GRAIN BASICS

WHAT ARE WHOLE GRAINS?

Whole grains are just that – grains that have been minimally processed so that all the nutritious parts of the seed remain intact. When the inedible hull is removed, the whole grain (a.k.a. the kernel, berry or groat) remains. It contains three components – the bran, the germ and the endosperm – each of which offers different vital nutrients (see opposite).

All grains start out whole. When they're made into refined ingredients (such as all-purpose, light rye or light buckwheat flour; pearl barley; or white rice), the germ and bran are removed and a significant amount of the nutrients is lost. Some vitamins and minerals, but not all, are added back to refined flours, but whole grain flours contain phytonutrients and fibre that can't be replaced.

Not all foods classified as "whole grains" are cereal grains like wheat, rye and oats. Some, such as quinoa, buckwheat, wild rice and amaranth, are actually seeds. They offer similar nutrients and behave like cereal grains in cooking, so they're included in this category. Because these seeds are not in the same family as cereal grains, they do not contain the protein gluten, making them versatile options for people with celiac disease (see page 13).

While eating only whole grains might be a noble goal, it's great to start by adding them to dishes you already love. Try whole grain pasta instead of white pasta one night, then give chewy kamut a try in your best pilaf recipe. It's all about balance and adding new and exciting flavours to your diet.

From top: Millet, kasha, kamut berries, wheat berries and wild rice

Bran The rough "skin" covering a whole grain, bran protects the kernel from damage by pests, the elements and diseases. It's an excellent source of insoluble fibre, which helps prevent constipation. It's also a source of B vitamins, antioxidants and minerals. Bran is discarded when grains are milled to make refined (white) flour.

Germ The embryo of the seed, the germ is the part that becomes a new plant when fertilized. It contains protein, vitamins, minerals and some healthy fat. Wheat germ is particularly nutritious and is commonly sold in supermarkets as a food supplement; it contains essential vitamins (notably vitamin E). The germ is discarded when making refined flour.

Endosperm The largest part of a whole grain, the endosperm lies under the bran and encloses the germ. This starchy area feeds the fertilized germ as it grows into a new plant. It's packed with carbohydrates and smaller amounts of vitamins, minerals and protein. This part of the kernel is made into refined flour.

Ever wonder where all that goodness comes from? Here's what a whole grain looks like inside and why each part is good for you.

ANATOMY OF A WHOLE GRAIN

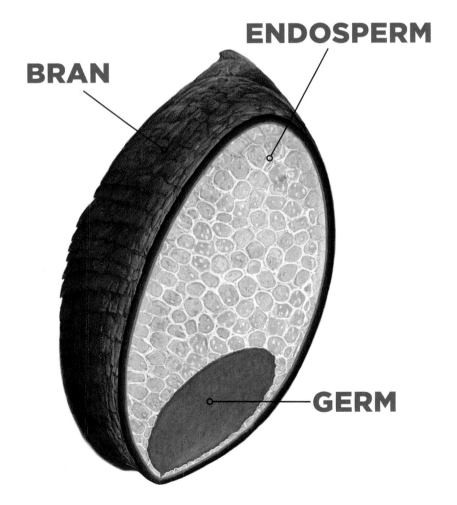

BRAN

ENDOSPERM

GERM

You've heard it a million times: Whole grains are good for you. But why, exactly? Here's the big picture on the nutrients you get from whole grains and the ways they help keep your body healthy and strong.

HEALTH BENEFITS OF WHOLE GRAINS

NUTRIENTS AT A GLANCE

Dietary fibre All whole grains are sources of insoluble fibre; oats, barley and amaranth are also sources of soluble fibre.

Vitamins Many grains are sources of B vitamins, such as thiamin, niacin, pyridoxine and folate.

Minerals Most grains are sources of magnesium and phosphorus; many are sources of other minerals, such as zinc, manganese, iron and selenium.

Protein Most whole grains are good sources of amino acids, the building blocks of protein; combining them with legumes creates complete proteins.

GOOD DIGESTION. Bran is a great source of insoluble fibre. This type of fibre bulks up stool, speeding it through your digestive system and keeping you regular. This helps your body eliminate toxins more quickly, protecting you from disease, and keeps you feeling comfortable.

LOWER CHOLESTEROL. Beta-glucan, a component of the soluble fibre found in oats and barley, can lower the level of bad cholesterol, or low-density lipoproteins (LDL), in the blood, potentially reducing your risk of heart disease.

STEADY BLOOD SUGAR. Unrefined grains break down more slowly than refined ones. These slow-release carbs don't cause blood sugar levels to rise quickly then plummet. This is particularly helpful for people with diabetes, who need to avoid spikes in blood sugar.

CANCER PREVENTION. Because insoluble fibre speeds up elimination, it helps carcinogens leave the digestive tract quickly, reducing your risk of colorectal cancer. Plus, the manganese and selenium found in some whole grains help defend your body against disease-causing free radicals.

BETTER IMMUNE FUNCTION. Since kamut, barley, whole wheat and brown rice are often noted for their selenium content, these grains provide a defence against free radicals, keeping your immune system in fighting shape.

LOWER STRESS. Most whole grains are good sources of B vitamins, which are often touted for their antistress properties. These vitamins also keep your metabolism moving along at a healthy pace.

There's no need to skip pastas and baked goods if you suffer from celiac disease. There are plenty of delicious options available for a gluten-free pantry. You'll also require some additives to help baked goods rise and achieve the proper texture, but they're increasingly easy to find.

GLUTEN-FREE WHOLE GRAINS

Gluten is a type of protein found in wheat, barley, rye, spelt, kamut and triticale. It can cause painful bloating, indigestion and diarrhea in people with celiac disease. If you suspect you have celiac disease, it's vital to consult a dietitian to avoid becoming malnourished.

But just because you have a gluten sensitivity doesn't mean you can't enjoy whole grains. A number of foods classified as whole grains are seeds that are not related to cereal grains. They contain no gluten and are tasty alternatives in many recipes.

The best strategy is to check every food label carefully for a gluten-free stamp. Many foods are also cross-contaminated with wheat during production. Avoid bulk bins (scoops are often shared between bins) and buy sealed packages that say the contents have been processed in a gluten-free facility.

PANTRY STAPLES

Amaranth Seeds and flour

Brown rice Grains, flour and pasta

Buckwheat Unroasted groats, kasha, dark buckwheat flour and pasta

Corn Cornmeal and popcorn

Millet Seeds and flour

Oats (pure uncontaminated) Groats, steel-cut oats, rolled oats and flour

Quinoa Seeds and flour

Wild rice Grains, flour and pasta

BAKING ADDITIVES

Potato starch Combine this bland, finely textured powder with rice flour to prevent an unpleasant grainy texture.

Tapioca starch Also called tapioca flour, cassava flour or cassava starch, this adds chewiness to baked goods when combined with other flours; it's especially important in breads.

Xanthan gum This is a substitute for gluten and provides structure in baked goods. It is expensive but stores well.

Gluten-free baking mixtures Also known as gluten-free all-purpose baking flour, these blends are best used according to package directions or in recipes designed around them.

Gluten-free baking powder Some health food stores carry baking powder that's labelled "gluten-free," but the regular kind is gluten-free in Canada too.

WHEAT, SPELT & KAMUT

Waffle irons are affordable and easy to use – perfect for any household with kids. Top these pecan-laced waffles with bananas in winter or fresh berries in summer, and serve with plenty of maple syrup.

WHOLE WHEAT PECAN WAFFLES

1 cup **all-purpose flour**

1 cup **whole wheat flour**

¼ cup **granulated sugar**

2 tsp **baking powder**

½ tsp **baking soda**

¼ tsp **salt**

2 **eggs**

2 cups **buttermilk**

¼ cup **butter,** melted

⅓ cup chopped **pecans**

2 tbsp **vegetable oil**

In large bowl, whisk together all-purpose and whole wheat flours, sugar, baking powder, baking soda and salt.

Whisk together eggs, buttermilk and butter; pour over flour mixture. Sprinkle with pecans and stir just until combined.

Heat waffle iron according to manufacturer's instructions. For each waffle, brush iron lightly with some of the oil; pour in ½ cup batter, spreading to edges. Close lid and cook until crisp, golden and steam stops, 4 to 6 minutes. *(Make-ahead: Let cool. Wrap individually and freeze in airtight container for up to 1 month. Reheat in toaster.)*

CHANGE IT UP

Whole Wheat Blueberry Waffles
Replace pecans with 1 cup fresh blueberries.

MAKES 8 WAFFLES. PER WAFFLE: about 310 cal, 8 g pro, 14 g total fat (6 g sat. fat), 39 g carb, 1 g fibre, 67 mg chol, 336 mg sodium. % RDI: 12% calcium, 14% iron, 8% vit A, 2% vit C, 34% folate.

Multigrain flour, rolled oats and wheat germ give these wholesome pancakes an appealing, toothsome texture. Multigrain flour is a combination of all-purpose and whole wheat flours, cracked wheat and rye, and whole flaxseeds. For a more delicate texture, substitute whole wheat flour for the multigrain.

BEST-EVER WHOLE GRAIN PANCAKES

2 cups **buttermilk**

¾ cup **quick-cooking rolled oats** (not instant)

¾ cup **multigrain flour**

¼ cup **natural raw wheat germ**

2 tbsp **granulated sugar**

1 tsp **baking powder**

1 tsp **baking soda**

½ tsp **salt**

1 **egg**

3 tbsp **vegetable oil**

TIP: If you don't have buttermilk, pour 2 tbsp vinegar or lemon juice into 2-cup glass measure. Pour in enough milk to make 2 cups. Let stand for 5 minutes; stir just before using.

Combine 1 cup of the buttermilk with oats; let stand for 10 minutes.

In large bowl, whisk together flour, wheat germ, sugar, baking powder, baking soda and salt. Whisk together remaining buttermilk, egg and 2 tbsp of the oil; add to dry ingredients along with oat mixture. Stir just until combined.

Lightly brush large nonstick skillet with some of the remaining oil; heat over medium heat. Using ¼ cup for each pancake, pour in batter, spreading with spatula to 4-inch (10 cm) diameter. Cook until underside is golden and bubbles break on top that don't fill in, about 2½ minutes.

Turn pancakes; cook until underside is golden, 1 to 2 minutes.

Repeat with remaining batter, brushing skillet with some of the remaining oil as needed between batches. *(Make-ahead: Let cool. Stack pancakes, separated by waxed paper, and freeze in resealable freezer bag for up to 2 weeks. Reheat in toaster.)*

MAKES 15 PANCAKES. PER PANCAKE: about 92 cal, 3 g pro, 4 g total fat (1 g sat. fat), 12 g carb, 1 g fibre, 14 mg chol, % RDI: 9% calcium, 44% iron, 1% vit A, 25% folate.

Hearty soups like this are a smart choice for feeding a hungry crowd. Kamut takes a while to simmer to a pleasantly chewy texture, so it's ideal for long-cooking soups like this. Stir in a couple of big pinches of chopped fresh parsley just before serving for a burst of fresh herb flavour.

BEEF & KAMUT SOUP

3 stems **fresh parsley**

1 **bay leaf**

3 sprigs **fresh thyme**

1½ lb (675 g) **stewing beef cubes,** cut in ½-inch (1 cm) cubes

¼ tsp each **salt** and **pepper**

2 tbsp **olive oil**

1 **onion,** diced

1 large **carrot,** diced

1 **parsnip,** diced

3 cloves **garlic,** chopped

2 tbsp **tomato paste**

1 tsp each **smoked paprika** and **ground cumin**

4 cups **sodium-reduced beef broth**

1 cup **kamut berries**

Place parsley stems, bay leaf and thyme on square of cheesecloth; tie tightly with kitchen string to form spice bag.

Toss together beef, salt and pepper. In Dutch oven, heat 4 tsp of the oil over high heat. Brown beef, in 2 batches, on all sides, about 10 minutes. Transfer to plate.

Add remaining oil to pan; heat over medium-high heat. Sauté onion, carrot, parsnip and garlic until softened, about 5 minutes. Stir in tomato paste, paprika and cumin; cook, stirring, until fragrant, about 1 minute.

Return beef and any accumulated juices to pan; add broth, 3 cups water, kamut and spice bag. Bring to boil; reduce heat and simmer, partially covered, until kamut is tender and soup is slightly thickened, about 1¾ hours. Discard spice bag.

TIP: Parsley stems usually get discarded, but they have lots of flavour and are great for seasoning soups.

MAKES ABOUT 6 SERVINGS. PER SERVING: about 400 cal, 30 g pro, 18 g total fat (6 g sat. fat), 32 g carb, 5 g fibre, 67 mg chol, 602 mg sodium, 713 mg potassium. % RDI: 5% calcium, 32% iron, 29% vit A, 10% vit C, 15% folate.

SPELT & KAMUT

These two grains are ancient forms of wheat. Spelt was a staple in medieval Europe. Kamut is the trademarked name for khorasan wheat, which is rumoured to have been found in Egyptian pharaohs' tombs; it was called "King Tut's wheat."

WHY THEY'RE GOOD FOR YOU: Some people who have trouble digesting wheat may have an easier time with spelt or kamut. However, both contain gluten and are not suitable for people with celiac disease. Spelt and kamut contain more protein than regular wheat, and offer healthy doses of fibre and minerals, such as selenium, zinc and magnesium.

WHOLE GRAIN FORMS: Spelt and kamut **berries** are the whole, unprocessed kernels of the plants. **Pasta** and **couscous** can be made from whole spelt or kamut flour, but be sure to read labels to ensure they're 100 per cent whole grain. Spelt and kamut **whole grain flours** give a complex, nutty taste to baked goods. These flours are often mixed with all-purpose flour to make breads and cakes rise.

STORAGE: The natural oils in these whole grain products can go rancid at room temperature, so freeze in airtight containers for best results.

USES: Try spelt and kamut flours in place of whole wheat flour in baked goods. The pasta and couscous can easily be substituted for the white-flour versions. Kamut berries are chewy and satisfying in soups and grain salads.

Clockwise from top left: Whole grain spelt flour, spelt penne pasta, spelt berries and kamut berries

Pantry staples plus fresh sweet peppers add up to a colourful, nutrient-packed weeknight dinner. Serve with grated or shaved Parmesan cheese to sprinkle over top.

WHOLE WHEAT PASTA WITH PEPPERS, TOMATOES & OLIVES

2 tbsp **extra-virgin olive oil**

3 **sweet peppers** (red, yellow and/or orange), thinly sliced

1 small **onion,** thinly sliced

2 cloves **garlic,** minced

1 tsp **dried marjoram** or dried thyme

¼ tsp each **salt** and **pepper**

Pinch **hot pepper flakes**

2 **plum tomatoes,** diced

¼ cup **oil-cured black olives,** halved and pitted

2 tbsp **cider vinegar** or wine vinegar

8 oz (225 g) **whole wheat spaghettini**

¼ cup chopped **fresh parsley**

In large skillet, heat oil over medium heat; fry sweet peppers, onion, garlic, marjoram, salt, pepper and hot pepper flakes, stirring often, until saucy and very tender, about 18 minutes.

Add tomatoes, olives and vinegar; cook, stirring, until heated through, about 1 minute.

Meanwhile, in large pot of boiling salted water, cook pasta according to package directions. Reserving ½ cup of the cooking liquid, drain pasta and return to pot.

Add pepper mixture and parsley to pasta; toss to coat, adding enough of the reserved cooking liquid to moisten.

MAKES 4 SERVINGS. PER SERVING: about 328 cal, 10 g pro, 11 g total fat (2 g sat. fat), 53 g carb, 7 g fibre, 0 mg chol, 638 mg sodium. % RDI: 5% calcium, 20% iron, 18% vit A, 242% vit C, 16% folate.

Meaty portobello mushrooms and toasted pine nuts give this dish an earthy, savoury flavour. Kamut pasta is a delicious complement to the sauce, but whole wheat pasta is just as tasty – and can be easier to find.

SPINACH, TOMATO & PORTOBELLO PASTA

3 tbsp **pine nuts**

3 tbsp **olive oil**

3 cloves **garlic,** minced

1 **shallot,** diced

2 large **portobello mushrooms,** stemmed, halved and thinly sliced

2 cups **grape tomatoes,** halved

12 oz (340 g) **kamut penne** or whole wheat penne

6 cups **fresh baby spinach**

2 tbsp **red wine vinegar**

½ tsp each **salt** and **pepper**

½ cup grated **Parmesan cheese**

In dry small skillet, toast pine nuts over medium-low heat until golden, about 4 minutes. Set aside.

In large skillet, heat oil over medium heat; cook garlic and shallot, stirring occasionally, until light golden, 3 to 4 minutes.

Add mushrooms; cook, stirring, until beginning to soften, about 4 minutes. Add tomatoes; cook over medium-high heat until skins begin to wrinkle, 1 to 2 minutes.

Meanwhile, in large pot of boiling salted water, cook pasta according to package directions. Reserving ½ cup of the cooking liquid, drain pasta and return to pot.

Stir in mushroom mixture, spinach, vinegar, salt, pepper, pine nuts and ¼ cup of the reserved cooking liquid, adding more liquid as needed to coat. Serve sprinkled with Parmesan cheese.

MAKES 4 SERVINGS. PER SERVING: about 520 cal, 21 g pro, 20 g total fat (4 g sat. fat), 72 g carb, 9 g fibre, 11 mg chol, 783 mg sodium, 712 mg potassium. % RDI: 23% calcium, 37% iron, 52% vit A, 20% vit C, 41% folate.

Macaroni and cheese is one of the best comfort food dishes around. But there's no reason you can't give it a healthy whole grain boost. Whole wheat pasta gives the dish a rich heartiness – and a dose of fibre.

WHOLE WHEAT MACARONI & CHEESE

12 oz (340 g) **button mushrooms**

1 tbsp **butter**

Pinch **salt**

1 pkg (375 g) **whole wheat elbow macaroni**

¾ cup **fresh bread crumbs**

2 tsp **olive oil**

CARAMELIZED ONIONS:

4 tsp **olive oil**

4 cups thinly sliced **onions**

¼ tsp **dried thyme**

1 **bay leaf**

Pinch **salt**

¼ cup **white wine** or water

CHEESE SAUCE:

3 tbsp **butter**

¼ cup **all-purpose flour**

1 tbsp **Dijon mustard**

3 cups **milk**

¼ tsp **salt**

Pinch **pepper**

1¾ cups shredded **Fontina cheese**

¾ cup shredded **old Cheddar cheese**

⅓ cup chopped **fresh parsley**

Cut mushrooms in half. In skillet, melt butter over medium-high heat; cook mushrooms and salt until browned and no liquid remains, 5 to 8 minutes. Transfer to bowl.

CARAMELIZED ONIONS: In same skillet, heat oil over medium-low heat; cook onions, thyme, bay leaf and salt, stirring, until caramelized and reduced to ¾ cup, 25 minutes. Stir in wine; cook, scraping up browned bits, until no liquid remains, 1 minute. Discard bay leaf. Add to mushrooms. *(Make-ahead: Let cool. Refrigerate in airtight container for up to 24 hours.)*

CHEESE SAUCE: Meanwhile, in saucepan, melt butter over medium heat; sprinkle with flour. Cook, stirring constantly, for 1 minute. Stir in mustard. Whisk in milk until smooth; bring to simmer.

Simmer, stirring, until thickened, 6 minutes. Sprinkle with salt and pepper; stir in Fontina cheese, Cheddar cheese and parsley until smooth. *(Make-ahead: Transfer to airtight container; place waxed paper directly on surface. Cover; refrigerate for up to 24 hours. Reheat, adding milk if necessary to thin.)*

Meanwhile, in large pot of boiling salted water, cook pasta until still slightly firm in centre, about 6 minutes. Drain and return to pot. Stir in cheese sauce and onion mixture. Transfer to greased 8-inch (2 L) square baking dish.

Combine bread crumbs with oil; sprinkle over pasta. Bake on baking sheet in 375°F (190°C) oven until bubbly and golden, about 30 minutes.

MAKES 4 TO 6 SERVINGS. PER EACH OF 6 SERVINGS: about 654 cal, 28 g pro, 31 g total fat (17 g sat. fat), 70 g carb, 8 g fibre, 83 mg chol, 797 mg sodium, 589 mg potassium. % RDI: 45% calcium, 26% iron, 28% vit A, 10% vit C, 25% folate.

We've lightened up this classic Italian meal by using extra-lean ground turkey instead of the usual beef and pork combination. Whole wheat pasta and bread crumbs give this dish a healthy hit of fibre that's not found in the traditional white-pasta version. Serve with a tossed green salad.

SMART SPAGHETTI & MEATBALLS

1¼ lb (565 g) **whole wheat spaghetti**

¼ cup torn **fresh basil leaves**

SAUCE:

1 tbsp **olive oil**

1 **carrot,** finely chopped

1 rib **celery,** finely chopped

Half small **sweet onion,** finely diced

3 cloves **garlic,** minced

½ tsp **dried Italian herb seasoning**

¼ tsp **salt**

¼ cup **dry white wine** or
  dry red wine

1 bottle (680 mL) **strained tomatoes**
  (passata)

MEATBALLS:

½ cup **fresh whole wheat
  bread crumbs**

1 **egg**

⅓ cup grated **Parmesan cheese**

2 cloves **garlic,** minced

½ tsp **dried Italian herb seasoning**

¼ tsp **salt**

Pinch **hot pepper flakes**

1 lb (450 g) **extra-lean ground
  turkey**

SAUCE: In saucepan, heat oil over medium heat; cook carrot, celery, onion, garlic, Italian seasoning and salt, stirring occasionally, until softened, about 7 minutes. Add wine; cook for 2 minutes. Add strained tomatoes and ¾ cup water; bring to boil. Reduce heat, cover and simmer, stirring occasionally, until slightly thickened, about 40 minutes.

MEATBALLS: Meanwhile, in large bowl, stir together bread crumbs, egg, Parmesan cheese, garlic, Italian seasoning, salt and hot pepper flakes; mix in turkey. Shape by scant 1 tbsp into 30 meatballs.

Bake on parchment paper–lined baking sheet in 375°F (190°C) oven until instant-read thermometer inserted into centre of several registers 165°F (74°C), about 15 minutes. Add to sauce.

Meanwhile, in large pot of boiling salted water, cook pasta according to package directions; drain. Serve topped with meatballs and sauce; garnish with basil.

MAKES 6 SERVINGS. PER SERVING: about 555 cal, 31 g pro, 13 g total fat (4 g sat. fat), 81 g carb, 9 g fibre, 90 mg chol, 881 mg sodium, 609 mg potassium. % RDI: 13% calcium, 46% iron, 25% vit A, 8% vit C, 17% folate.

The heavenly pairing of creamy blue cheese and toasted walnuts is delicious with whole wheat pasta. This dish is special enough for company but is still easy comfort food you can enjoy on a quiet weeknight.

WHOLE WHEAT LINGUINE WITH BLUE CHEESE SAUCE

½ cup **milk**

½ cup crumbled **blue cheese** (about 4 oz/115 g)

⅓ cup grated **Parmesan cheese**

¼ cup **whipping cream** (35%)

1 tbsp **butter**

Pinch **salt**

⅓ cup chopped **fresh parsley**

12 oz (340 g) **whole wheat linguine**

3 tbsp chopped **walnuts**, toasted

In saucepan, combine milk, blue cheese, Parmesan cheese, cream, butter and salt; cook over medium heat, stirring often, until thickened, about 5 minutes. Stir in parsley; keep warm.

Meanwhile, in large pot of boiling salted water, cook pasta according to package directions. Reserving ¼ cup of the cooking liquid, drain pasta and return to pot.

Add sauce; toss to coat. Stir in enough of the reserved cooking liquid to keep sauce loose and creamy. Serve sprinkled with walnuts.

MAKES 4 SERVINGS. PER SERVING: about 559 cal, 24 g pro, 24 g total fat (13 g sat. fat), 67 g carb, 8 g fibre, 58 mg chol, 832 mg sodium. % RDI: 31% calcium, 23% iron, 20% vit A, 10% vit C, 16% folate.

This vegetarian burger has a substantial feel and meaty texture thanks to the mushrooms and bulgur (a whole grain form of wheat commonly used in Middle Eastern cuisine); you'll never miss the beef. Serve the patties on whole wheat kaiser rolls with lettuce, tomato and your favourite burger fixings.

BULGUR & MUSHROOM BURGERS

1 cup **boiling water**

¾ cup **bulgur** (medium or coarse)

1 **egg,** beaten

1 cup **fresh whole wheat bread crumbs**

¼ cup minced **fresh parsley**

8 oz (225 g) **mushrooms**

2 tbsp **extra-virgin olive oil**

1 small **onion,** finely chopped

2 cloves **garlic,** minced

¼ cup **dry white wine** or vegetable broth

½ tsp **salt**

¼ tsp **pepper**

¼ tsp **dried thyme**

In heatproof bowl, pour boiling water over bulgur; let stand until doubled in bulk, 20 minutes. Mix in egg, bread crumbs and parsley.

Meanwhile, roughly break mushrooms into pieces; in food processor, pulse until finely chopped. In skillet, heat oil over medium heat; fry onion and garlic until softened, about 3 minutes. Stir in mushrooms, wine, salt, pepper and thyme; cook over medium-high heat, stirring occasionally, until no liquid remains and mushrooms begin to brown, about 8 minutes.

Mix into bulgur mixture. Shape into four ¾-inch (2 cm) thick patties. Place on greased grill over medium heat; close lid and grill, turning once, until heated through and crispy, about 15 minutes.

MAKES 4 BURGERS. PER BURGER: about 220 cal, 7 g pro, 9 g total fat (1 g sat. fat), 30 g carb, 5 g fibre, 47 mg chol, 370 mg sodium. % RDI: 4% calcium, 19% iron, 4% vit A, 12% vit C, 20% folate.

Parchment packets seal in moisture so fish stays juicy as it cooks. The couscous will soak up some of the juices from the fish on top, giving it extra flavour.

SALMON & COUSCOUS IN PARCHMENT

2 tbsp finely chopped **fresh parsley**

2 tbsp **extra-virgin olive oil**

1 tbsp **wine vinegar**

2 tsp **Dijon mustard**

1 tsp **dried oregano**

1 **green onion,** thinly sliced

1 clove **garlic,** minced

½ tsp each **salt** and **pepper**

1 cup **whole wheat couscous**

1 cup **boiling water**

3 tbsp chopped drained **oil-packed sun-dried tomatoes**

4 **skinless salmon fillets** or skinless trout fillets (about 1½ lb/675 g total)

4 **lemon wedges**

In large bowl, whisk together parsley, oil, vinegar, mustard, oregano, green onion, garlic, salt and pepper. Remove 2 tbsp; set aside for serving.

Into remaining oil mixture, stir couscous, boiling water and tomatoes; cover and let stand for 5 minutes. Fluff with fork.

Cut four 12-inch (30 cm) squares of parchment paper. Evenly spoon couscous onto 1 half of each square; top each with fish fillet. Fold paper over so edges meet; fold and pinch all open edges together to seal packets.

Place packets on rimmed baking sheet. Bake in 400°F (200°C) oven until fish flakes easily when tested, about 17 minutes. Open packets; drizzle with reserved oil mixture. Serve with lemon wedges.

MAKES 4 SERVINGS. PER SERVING: about 479 cal, 40 g pro, 18 g total fat (4 g sat. fat), 41 g carb, 6 g fibre, 90 mg chol, 393 mg sodium. % RDI: 13% calcium, 18% iron, 13% vit A, 27% vit C, 17% folate.

Whole wheat couscous is a delicious alternative to rice or bread in stuffings. This stuffing is gently spiced, and the orange and currants add a sweet accent.

COUSCOUS CHICKEN WITH ORANGE SAUCE

2 tbsp **vegetable oil**

1 **onion,** thinly sliced

2 cloves **garlic,** minced

1 tsp each **sweet paprika** and **ground cumin**

½ tsp each **salt** and **pepper**

Pinch each **cinnamon** and **cayenne pepper**

⅓ cup **whole wheat couscous**

⅓ cup **boiling water**

½ cup **orange juice**

2 tbsp **dried currants**

¼ cup chopped **fresh parsley**

2 tbsp **sliced almonds**

4 **boneless skinless chicken breasts**

1 tsp cold **water**

¼ tsp **cornstarch**

In skillet, heat half of the oil over medium heat; cook onion, garlic, paprika, cumin, half each of the salt and pepper, the cinnamon and cayenne pepper until onion is softened, about 6 minutes.

Meanwhile, place couscous in heatproof bowl; pour boiling water over top. Stir in half of the orange juice and the currants. Cover and let stand until no liquid remains, about 5 minutes. Fluff with fork; stir in onion mixture, parsley and almonds.

With knife parallel to cutting board, cut each chicken breast in half horizontally almost but not all the way through; open like a book. Top half with couscous mixture; fold uncovered half over couscous. Skewer shut. Place in roasting pan; brush with remaining oil. Sprinkle with remaining salt and pepper.

Roast in 400°F (200°C) oven until chicken is no longer pink inside, about 20 minutes. Transfer to plate; keep warm.

Strain pan juices into saucepan; add remaining orange juice and bring to boil. Stir cold water with cornstarch; stir into sauce and boil until glossy and thickened, about 1 minute. Serve over chicken.

MAKES 4 SERVINGS. PER SERVING: about 332 cal, 34 g pro, 11 g total fat (1 g sat. fat), 24 g carb, 4 g fibre, 77 mg chol, 367 mg sodium, 624 mg potassium. % RDI: 4% calcium, 16% iron, 7% vit A, 30% vit C, 12% folate.

While Cubanelle peppers, zucchini and whole wheat tortillas are not traditional Tex-Mex ingredients, their flavours give this lasagna-style casserole a modern kick and some extra fibre.

TEX-MEX CASSEROLE WITH MONTEREY JACK

1 can (28 oz/796 mL) **whole tomatoes**

1 tbsp **extra-virgin olive oil**

2 **onions,** chopped

2 **Cubanelle peppers,** chopped

2 lb (900 g) **lean ground beef**

2 cloves **garlic,** minced

2 tbsp **chili powder**

1 tbsp **cumin seeds,** crushed

½ tsp each **salt** and **pepper**

¼ tsp **hot pepper flakes**

3 tbsp **tomato paste**

2 cups chopped **zucchini**

⅔ cup **sodium-reduced beef broth**

6 large (10-inch/25 cm) **whole wheat tortillas**

3½ cups shredded **Monterey Jack cheese** (9 oz/255 g)

Reserving juice, drain tomatoes; chop. Set both aside.

In large saucepan, heat oil over medium heat; cook onions and peppers, stirring occasionally, until softened, about 7 minutes.

Push mixture to side of pan. Add beef to other side; brown over medium-high heat, breaking up with back of spoon, about 4 minutes.

Stir in garlic, chili powder, cumin seeds, salt, pepper and hot pepper flakes. Stir in tomato paste; cook for 1 minute. Stir in reserved tomatoes and juice, zucchini and broth; simmer, stirring occasionally, for 20 minutes. Let cool.

Spread 1 cup of the beef mixture in 13- x 9-inch (3 L) baking dish. Top with 2 tortillas, then generous 2 cups of the beef mixture; sprinkle with one-third of the cheese. Starting with tortillas, repeat layers twice. *(Make-ahead: Cover with plastic wrap and overwrap in heavy-duty foil; freeze for up to 2 months. Thaw in refrigerator for 24 hours; remove plastic wrap and re-cover with foil. Increase baking time to 30 minutes; uncover and bake for 15 minutes more. Broil and let stand as directed.)*

Cover with foil. Bake in 400°F (200°C) oven until knife inserted in centre comes out hot, about 25 minutes. Uncover and broil until cheese is browned, about 4 minutes. Let stand for 10 minutes before serving.

MAKES 8 TO 10 SERVINGS. PER EACH OF 10 SERVINGS: about 453 cal, 34 g pro, 24 g total fat (11 g sat. fat), 26 g carb, 4 g fibre, 85 mg chol, 828 mg sodium, 651 mg potassium. % RDI: 33% calcium, 32% iron, 17% vit A, 35% vit C, 18% folate.

Chewy wheat berries and tender black beans are fibre-packed and make a delicious base for a filling salad. Avocado adds a delicious creamy note, but it does increase the fat content; if this is a concern, just leave it out.

BEAN & GRAIN SALAD WITH CILANTRO CHILI DRESSING

½ cup **soft wheat berries**

1 can (19 oz/540 mL) **black beans,** drained and rinsed

1 cup halved **cherry tomatoes** or grape tomatoes

1 each **sweet red pepper** and **sweet yellow pepper,** diced

2 **green onions,** thinly sliced

1 **avocado** (optional), peeled, pitted and cubed

½ cup crumbled **feta cheese**

3 cups torn **romaine lettuce**

1 cup shredded **kale**

CILANTRO CHILI DRESSING:

2 tbsp chopped **fresh cilantro**

2 tbsp each **extra-virgin olive oil** and **canola oil**

2 tbsp **cider vinegar**

1 tbsp minced **shallot**

1 small clove **garlic,** minced

1 tsp minced **hot pepper**

Pinch each **salt** and **pepper**

Bring large saucepan of salted water to boil. Add wheat berries; cover and simmer over medium-low heat until tender, 45 to 60 minutes. Drain and transfer to large bowl; let cool for about 15 minutes.

CILANTRO CHILI DRESSING: Whisk together cilantro, olive oil, canola oil, vinegar, shallot, garlic, hot pepper, salt and pepper.

To wheat berries, add black beans, tomatoes, red pepper, yellow pepper, green onions, avocado (if using) and feta cheese; add dressing and toss to coat.

Divide lettuce and kale among 4 plates; top with salad.

TIP: Pearled (polished) wheat berries are rubbed to remove the bran, so they're not a whole grain. They do work in this recipe; just reduce the cooking time to 25 minutes.

MAKES 4 SERVINGS. PER SERVING: about 379 cal, 14 g pro, 19 g total fat (5 g sat. fat), 44 g carb, 13 g fibre, 17 mg chol, 655 mg sodium. % RDI: 17% calcium, 27% iron, 53% vit A, 250% vit C, 66% folate.

This is the classic salad served all over the Middle East alongside grilled meats or as part of an assortment of small dishes called *mezze*. Fresh herbs are the key to its sunny, summery flavour.

TABBOULEH SALAD

1 cup **bulgur** (medium or coarse)

1 can (19 oz/540 mL) **chickpeas,** drained and rinsed

2 **tomatoes,** seeded and chopped

1 cup diced **English cucumber**

1 cup minced **fresh flat-leaf parsley**

½ cup chopped **green onions**

¼ cup chopped **fresh mint**

DRESSING:

¼ cup **lemon juice**

2 tbsp **extra-virgin olive oil**

2 cloves **garlic,** minced

1 tsp **salt**

½ tsp **pepper**

In saucepan, bring 1¾ cups water to boil; stir in bulgur. Cover and cook over low heat until no liquid remains, about 10 minutes. Transfer to large bowl; fluff with fork. Let cool to room temperature.

Add chickpeas, tomatoes, cucumber, parsley, green onions and mint.

DRESSING: Whisk together lemon juice, oil, garlic, salt and pepper; pour over bulgur mixture. Toss to combine.

MAKES 4 SERVINGS. PER SERVING: about 336 cal, 13 g pro, 9 g total fat (1 g sat. fat), 56 g carb, 9 g fibre, 0 mg chol, 803 mg sodium. % RDI: 8% calcium, 29% iron, 14% vit A, 60% vit C, 56% folate.

Flecked with bits of red pepper, pale cheese and green parsley, this salad is as pretty to look at as it is delicious to eat. You can use soft wheat berries instead of the hard; reduce their cooking time by 15 minutes.

CURRIED WHEAT BERRY SALAD

1½ cups **hard wheat berries**

¼ cup **pine nuts** or slivered almonds

3 tbsp **vegetable oil**

1 **onion,** chopped

2 cloves **garlic,** minced

1 tbsp **mild curry paste**

¼ tsp **salt**

3 tbsp **white wine vinegar**

1 **sweet red pepper,** diced

½ cup cubed **cumin Gouda cheese** or mozzarella cheese

2 tbsp chopped **fresh parsley**

In large saucepan of boiling salted water, cover and cook wheat berries until tender but firm to the bite, 45 to 60 minutes. Drain well. Transfer to large bowl.

Meanwhile, in dry large skillet, toast pine nuts over medium heat until golden, about 2 minutes. Transfer to small bowl; set aside.

In same skillet, heat 1 tbsp of the oil over medium heat; fry onion and garlic, stirring often, for 2 minutes. Add curry paste and salt; fry, stirring, until onion is softened, about 3 minutes. Remove from heat. Stir in remaining oil and vinegar. Add to wheat berries; toss to coat. Let cool. *(Make-ahead: Cover and refrigerate for up to 2 days.)*

Add pine nuts, red pepper, Gouda cheese and parsley; toss to combine.

CHANGE IT UP
Curried Barley Salad
Replace wheat berries with pot barley.

MAKES 4 TO 6 SERVINGS. PER EACH OF 6 SERVINGS: about 305 cal, 9 g pro, 15 g total fat (3 g sat. fat), 36 g carb, 7 g fibre, 13 mg chol, 708 mg sodium. % RDI: 9% calcium, 16% iron, 9% vit A, 57% vit C, 11% folate.

Clockwise from top left:
Soft wheat berries, hard
wheat berries, coarse bulgur
and whole wheat couscous

WHEAT

WHY IT'S GOOD FOR YOU: Whole wheat products contain all of the wheat kernel – bran, germ and endosperm – so they're high in fibre and nutrients. They're excellent sources of selenium and magnesium, and good sources of phosphorus, all of which are essential minerals. You'll also get iron and some B vitamins in whole wheat foods.

WHOLE GRAIN FORMS: Wheat **berries** are the unprocessed kernels of the wheat plant. They come in soft and hard varieties (hard takes longer to cook). **Bulgur** is made by removing a small portion of the bran, but it is still considered a whole grain. It comes in coarse and fine grinds. **Whole wheat flour** that's labelled "100 per cent whole grain" or "stone-ground" contains all parts of the wheat kernel, so it's highly nutritious. Check labels carefully, as many whole wheat flours are not 100 per cent whole grain. Some whole wheat flours contain added gluten for bread baking. **Pasta** and **couscous** made from whole wheat flour are widely available in supermarkets.

STORAGE: The natural oils in whole wheat can spoil at room temperature. Keep flour, bulgur and wheat berries in the freezer; pasta, couscous and other dried products are fine in the pantry.

USES: Whole wheat flour is excellent in breads, cookies, muffins and other baked goods. It's also deliciously nutty in crumb or crumble toppings on desserts. Whole wheat pasta has a robust taste that's good with flavourful sauces. Couscous, bulgur and wheat berries make tasty grain salads.

A tangy spiced vinaigrette gives this salad a touch of smokiness that complements the sweet corn and red pepper. Serve it with your favourite grilled or roasted pork dish.

WHEAT BERRY, CORN & RED PEPPER SALAD

1 cup **soft wheat berries**

1 cup **frozen corn kernels**

1 **sweet red pepper,** diced

4 **green onions,** sliced

5 leaves **fresh basil,** finely shredded

SMOKED PAPRIKA VINAIGRETTE:

3 tbsp **white wine vinegar**

1 clove **garlic,** minced

1 tsp **Dijon mustard**

½ tsp **smoked paprika**

¼ tsp each **salt** and **pepper**

3 tbsp **vegetable oil**

SMOKED PAPRIKA VINAIGRETTE:
In large bowl, whisk together vinegar, garlic, mustard, paprika, salt and pepper; gradually whisk in oil. Set aside.

In saucepan of boiling salted water, cook wheat berries until tender, about 1 hour. Add corn; cook for 30 seconds. Drain and rinse under cold water; drain again and add to vinaigrette.

Add red pepper, green onions and basil; toss to combine. Cover and refrigerate for 1 hour. *(Make-ahead: Refrigerate for up to 24 hours.)*

MAKES 8 SERVINGS. PER SERVING: about 149 cal, 4 g pro, 6 g total fat (1 g sat. fat), 23 g carb, 4 g fibre, 0 mg chol, 506 mg sodium, 188 mg potassium. % RDI: 2% calcium, 8% iron, 7% vit A, 43% vit C, 9% folate.

Mediterranean flavours are the order of the day in this hearty pasta salad. Rotini is the ideal choice because its spirals pick up and hold on to the delicious chunky vegetables and dressing.

GRILLED VEGETABLE PASTA SALAD

⅓ cup each chopped **fresh parsley** and **fresh basil**

⅓ cup **extra-virgin olive oil**

¼ cup **red wine vinegar** or white wine vinegar

1 clove **garlic,** minced

½ tsp each **salt** and **pepper**

2 **portobello mushrooms,** stemmed and gills removed

1 **red onion,** cut in ½-inch (1 cm) thick rounds

1 **zucchini,** cut lengthwise in ¼-inch (5 mm) thick strips

12 oz (340 g) **whole wheat rotini** (4 cups)

2 cups **cherry tomatoes,** halved

1 jar (6 oz/175 mL) **marinated artichoke hearts,** drained and rinsed

⅓ cup sliced **pimiento-stuffed olives**

¼ cup shaved **Parmesan cheese**

In large bowl, whisk together parsley, basil, oil, vinegar, garlic, salt and pepper; set aside.

Place mushrooms, onion and zucchini on greased grill over medium-high heat; close lid and grill, turning once, until tender-crisp, 5 to 10 minutes.

Cut mushrooms and onion into ½-inch (1 cm) chunks. Cut zucchini crosswise into ½-inch (1 cm) wide slices. Add vegetables to bowl; toss to coat.

Meanwhile, in large pot of boiling salted water, cook pasta according to package directions. Drain and rinse; drain well.

Add pasta, tomatoes, artichokes and olives to vegetable mixture; toss to combine. Sprinkle with Parmesan cheese.

MAKES 4 SERVINGS. PER SERVING: about 613 cal, 21 g pro, 26 g total fat (4 g sat. fat), 83 g carb, 14 g fibre, 5 mg chol, 844 mg sodium. % RDI: 16% calcium, 32% iron, 19% vit A, 37% vit C, 35% folate.

Couscous is a tasty base for salads. The dressing for this one is infused with ready-made pesto, which gives it a delicious herbal flavour without the work of making your own pesto from scratch.

GRILLED VEGETABLE COUSCOUS SALAD

3 tbsp **balsamic vinegar**

2 tbsp **pesto**

1 tbsp **extra-virgin olive oil**

½ tsp **pepper**

¾ cup **whole wheat couscous**

¾ cup **boiling water**

1 can (19 oz/540 mL) **chickpeas,** drained and rinsed

1 **green onion,** sliced

1 **eggplant**

1 **zucchini**

1 **sweet yellow pepper,** quartered

1 cup halved **grape tomatoes** or cherry tomatoes

Whisk together vinegar, pesto, oil and pepper; set aside.

In large heatproof bowl, combine couscous with boiling water; cover and let stand for 5 minutes. Fluff with fork; fold in chickpeas and green onion.

Cut eggplant and zucchini lengthwise into ¼-inch (5 mm) thick slices. Place eggplant, zucchini and yellow pepper on greased grill over medium-high heat; close lid and grill, turning once, until tender-crisp, about 10 minutes.

Cut eggplant and zucchini into 1-inch (2.5 cm) wide strips. Cut pepper into 1-inch (2.5 cm) pieces. Add grilled vegetables and tomatoes to couscous mixture. Add pesto mixture; toss to combine.

MAKES 4 SERVINGS. PER SERVING: about 395 cal, 13 g pro, 8 g total fat (1 g sat. fat), 72 g carb, 14 g fibre, 0 mg chol, 385 mg sodium. % RDI: 7% calcium, 24% iron, 11% vit A, 93% vit C, 45% folate.

The bacon fat in this dressing will solidify after a while, especially when leftovers are stored in the refrigerator. To reliquefy the dressing, microwave the salad at high, 30 seconds at a time and stirring after each heating, until dressing becomes warm and liquid again.

KAMUT SALAD WITH WARM BACON VINAIGRETTE

1½ cups **kamut berries**

1 tsp **olive oil**

2 cloves **garlic,** minced

6 cups packed **fresh baby spinach**

4 slices thick-cut **bacon**

3 tbsp **white wine vinegar**

2 tbsp chopped **fresh basil**

2 tbsp **lemon juice**

1 **shallot,** minced

1 tbsp **grainy mustard**

1 tbsp **liquid honey**

Pinch each **salt** and **pepper**

1 cup **grape tomatoes,** halved

In large saucepan of boiling water, cook kamut until tender but still firm, about 1¼ hours. Drain and set aside. *(Make-ahead: Cover and refrigerate for up to 2 days.)*

In large skillet, heat oil over medium-high heat; sauté garlic until fragrant, about 2 minutes. Add spinach; cook, stirring, until wilted, 3 to 5 minutes. Set aside.

Wipe out skillet; cook bacon over medium-high heat, turning often, until crisp, about 10 minutes. Reserving fat, drain bacon on paper towel–lined plate. Keep bacon fat warm; chop bacon.

In large bowl, whisk together vinegar, basil, lemon juice, shallot, mustard, honey, salt and pepper. Whisk in reserved bacon fat. Add tomatoes, spinach mixture, bacon and kamut; toss until coated.

MAKES 6 TO 8 SERVINGS. PER EACH OF 8 SERVINGS: about 238 cal, 8 g pro, 11 g total fat (4 g sat. fat), 29 g carb, 4 g fibre, 12 mg chol, 151 mg sodium, 350 mg potassium. % RDI: 4% calcium, 19% iron, 25% vit A, 8% vit C, 20% folate.

Lentils add protein and fibre to an already healthy, nutrient-rich couscous salad. Smaller portions make a nice side to pair with grilled foods, while larger portions make a delicious vegetarian main dish.

GRILLED VEGETABLE LENTIL COUSCOUS SALAD

2 cloves **garlic,** minced

¾ tsp **salt**

⅓ cup **extra-virgin olive oil**

3 tbsp **lemon juice**

½ tsp each **ground cumin** and **ground coriander**

2 each **zucchini** and **portobello mushrooms**

1 each **sweet red pepper** and **sweet yellow pepper**

½ cup **dried green lentils**

1 cup **whole wheat couscous**

1 cup **boiling water**

⅓ cup minced **fresh cilantro**

⅓ cup crumbled **feta cheese**

On cutting board and using side of chef's knife or fork, mash garlic with salt until smooth paste forms. In small bowl, combine garlic mixture, oil, lemon juice, cumin and coriander. Set aside.

Cut zucchini lengthwise into ½-inch (1 cm) thick slices. Remove mushroom stems. Seed and quarter red and yellow peppers. Brush vegetables with 2 tbsp of the oil mixture.

Place on greased grill over medium heat; close lid and grill, turning often, until tender, about 6 minutes for zucchini and 10 minutes for peppers and mushrooms. Let cool; coarsely chop.

Meanwhile, in saucepan of boiling salted water, cook lentils until tender, about 20 minutes. Drain and set aside.

In large heatproof bowl, combine couscous and boiling water; cover and let stand until absorbed, about 5 minutes. Fluff with fork. Add lentils, vegetables, cilantro, feta cheese and remaining oil mixture; toss to combine.

MAKES 4 SERVINGS. PER SERVING: about 511 cal, 19 g pro, 23 g total fat (5 g sat. fat), 65 g carb, 13 g fibre, 11 mg chol, 671 mg sodium, 1,023 mg potassium. % RDI: 11% calcium, 38% iron, 23% vit A, 168% vit C, 78% folate.

Bran muffins are a tasty way to jump-start your fibre intake in the morning. The flaxseeds and cranberries add nice contrasting textures to these tender treats.

BRAN FLAXSEED CRANBERRY MUFFINS

1⅓ cups **buttermilk**

¾ cup **All-Bran** or 100% Bran cereal

½ cup **natural bran**

⅔ cup **fancy molasses**

⅓ cup **vegetable oil**

1 **egg**

1½ tsp **vanilla**

2 cups **all-purpose flour**

¾ cup **whole wheat flour**

½ cup packed **dark brown sugar**

¼ cup **flaxseeds**

4 tsp **baking powder**

2 tsp **baking soda**

¼ tsp each **nutmeg** and **salt**

1 cup **dried cranberries**

In bowl, stir together buttermilk, All-Bran and natural bran; let stand for 10 minutes. Stir together molasses, oil, egg and vanilla; stir into bran mixture.

In large bowl, whisk together all-purpose and whole wheat flours, sugar, flaxseeds, baking powder, baking soda, nutmeg and salt. Pour bran mixture over top. Sprinkle with cranberries; stir just until moistened.

Scoop scant ½ cup into each of 12 greased or paper-lined muffin cups. Bake in 375°F (190°C) oven until firm to the touch, about 25 minutes.

Let cool in pan on rack for 2 minutes; transfer to rack and let cool. *(Make-ahead: Store in airtight container for up to 2 days. Or wrap separately in plastic wrap; freeze in airtight container for up to 2 weeks.)*

MAKES 12 MUFFINS. PER MUFFIN: about 475 cal, 9 g pro, 13 g total fat (1 g sat. fat), 87 g carb, 9 g fibre, 25 mg chol, 617 mg sodium. % RDI: 19% calcium, 37% iron, 1% vit A, 5% vit C, 30% folate.

Natural raw wheat germ is unprocessed and should be kept in the freezer to prevent the oils in it from going rancid. Look for it in natural food stores and large supermarkets. If you can't find it, try toasted wheat germ, which is crunchier; it's usually simply labelled "wheat germ."

FIG & PECAN MUFFINS

1½ cups **all-purpose flour**

½ cup **natural bran**

½ cup **natural raw wheat germ** or wheat germ

2 tsp **baking powder**

½ tsp **baking soda**

¼ tsp each **salt** and **nutmeg**

1 cup **pecan pieces**

1 cup finely chopped **Calimyrna figs**

½ cup **maple syrup**

⅓ cup **light-tasting olive oil** or safflower oil

2 tbsp packed **brown sugar**

2 **eggs**

1⅓ cups **buttermilk**

Whisk together flour, wheat bran, wheat germ, baking powder, baking soda, salt and nutmeg; stir in pecans and figs.

In large bowl, whisk together maple syrup, oil, brown sugar and eggs; whisk in buttermilk. Stir in flour mixture just until combined. Spoon into 12 paper-lined or greased muffin cups.

Bake in 375°F (190°C) oven until firm to the touch, about 25 minutes.

Let cool in pan on rack for 2 minutes; transfer to rack and let cool. (*Make-ahead: Store in airtight container for up to 2 days. Or wrap separately in plastic wrap; freeze in airtight container for up to 2 weeks.*)

✳TIP: Dried Calimyrna figs are golden, subtly sweet and a good source of fibre, but any dried fig will work in these tasty muffins.

MAKES 12 MUFFINS. PER MUFFIN: about 303 cal, 7 g pro, 15 g total fat (2 g sat. fat), 39 g carb, 5 g fibre, 33 mg chol, 189 mg sodium, 323 mg potassium. % RDI: 10% calcium, 16% iron, 2% vit A, 3% vit C, 23% folate.

Quick and easy to make, these biscuit fingers are wonderful with soups and stews. Or you can enjoy them as a snack with honey or hummus.

THREE-SEED BISCUITS

1¼ cups **all-purpose flour**

1 cup **whole wheat flour**

¼ cup **sunflower seeds**

¼ cup **flaxseeds**

¼ cup **natural raw wheat germ**

1 tbsp **granulated sugar**

1 tbsp **baking powder**

½ tsp **salt**

½ cup cold **butter,** cubed

1 cup **milk**

1 **egg,** lightly beaten

2 tbsp **sesame seeds**

In large bowl, whisk together all-purpose and whole wheat flours, sunflower seeds, flaxseeds, wheat germ, sugar, baking powder and salt. Using pastry blender or 2 knives, cut in butter until in coarse crumbs. Stir in milk to form soft, slightly sticky dough.

Turn out onto lightly floured surface; with floured hands, knead gently 10 times. Pat into 7-inch (18 cm) square. Cut into quarters; cut each quarter into 3 strips. Place, 1 inch (2.5 cm) apart, on ungreased rimmed baking sheet. Brush tops with egg; sprinkle with sesame seeds.

Bake in 425°F (220°C) oven until golden, about 12 minutes. Let cool on pan on rack.

MAKES 12 BISCUITS. PER BISCUIT: about 225 cal, 6 g pro, 13 g total fat (6 g sat. fat), 23 g carb, 3 g fibre, 37 mg chol, 242 mg sodium. % RDI: 8% calcium, 13% iron, 8% vit A, 25% folate.

Goat cheese adds a little tang to these rustic biscuits. They can partner with sweet toppings, such as jam and honey, as well as savoury main dishes.

GOAT CHEESE SPELT BISCUITS

1¼ cups **all-purpose flour**

¾ cup **whole spelt flour**

1 tbsp **baking powder**

1 tsp **granulated sugar**

½ tsp **salt**

½ cup cold **unsalted butter,** cubed

¾ cup **milk**

¾ cup crumbled **goat cheese** (3 oz/85 g)

In large bowl, whisk together all-purpose flour, spelt flour, baking powder, sugar and salt. Using pastry blender or 2 knives, cut in butter until crumbly. Pour all but 1 tbsp of the milk over top; sprinkle with goat cheese. Stir with fork to form soft ragged dough.

Turn out onto lightly floured surface; with floured hands, knead gently 10 times. Pat or roll out to ½-inch (1 cm) thickness. Using floured 2½-inch (6 cm) round cutter, cut out biscuits, pressing scraps together and cutting to make final biscuit. Place on parchment paper–lined or flour-dusted rimmed baking sheet.

Brush tops with remaining milk. Bake in 400°F (200°C) oven until golden, 18 to 20 minutes. Transfer to rack; let cool.

MAKES ABOUT 15 BISCUITS. PER BISCUIT: about 140 cal, 3 g pro, 8 g total fat (5 g sat. fat), 14 g carb, 1 g fibre, 20 mg chol, 164 mg sodium, 35 mg potassium. % RDI: 5% calcium, 4% iron, 8% vit A, 10% folate.

Sweet and a little salty, this ultrasimple spread is delicious on all sorts of homemade whole grain treats: scones, breads and especially Multigrain Biscuits (opposite).

HONEY BUTTER

⅓ cup **butter,** softened

2 tbsp **liquid honey**

In small bowl and using fork, mash butter with honey until smooth. *(Make-ahead: Refrigerate in airtight container for up to 1 week; let come to room temperature before using.)*

MAKES ABOUT ½ CUP. PER 1 TBSP: about 84 cal, trace pro, 8 g total fat (5 g sat. fat), 4 g carb, 0 g fibre, 20 mg chol, 55 mg sodium. % RDI: 7% vit A.

This creamy spread pairs especially well with dark whole grain baked goods, such as Pumpernickel Bread (page 146) and Whole Wheat & Rye Cracker Bread (page 156).

BLUE CHEESE BUTTER

¼ cup **butter,** softened

½ cup cold crumbled **blue cheese**

In small bowl, beat butter until fluffy. Fold in cheese to make chunky spread. *(Make-ahead: Refrigerate in airtight container for up to 1 week; let come to room temperature before using.)*

MAKES ABOUT ½ CUP. PER 1 TBSP: about 81 cal, 2 g pro, 8 g total fat (5 g sat. fat), trace carb, 0 g fibre, 22 mg chol, 159 mg sodium. % RDI: 4% calcium, 7% vit A, 1% folate.

With double the fibre of white flour, multigrain flour offers more nutritional value and has a delicious, nutty flavour. A small cutter makes dainty biscuits that are perfect for dollops of summer-fresh jam.

MULTIGRAIN BISCUITS

2 cups **multigrain flour** (such as Robin Hood Best for Bread Multigrain Blend)

2 tbsp packed **brown sugar**

2 tsp **baking powder**

½ tsp each **baking soda** and **salt**

¼ cup cold **butter,** cubed

1 cup **buttermilk**

1 **egg,** lightly beaten

In large bowl, whisk together multigrain flour, brown sugar, baking powder, baking soda and salt. Using pastry blender or 2 knives, cut in butter until crumbly. Pour in buttermilk; stir with fork to make soft ragged dough.

With lightly floured hands, press dough into ball. On lightly floured surface, gently knead 10 times. Pat into ¾-inch (2 cm) thick round. Using floured 2-inch (5 cm) round cutter, cut out biscuits, pressing scraps together and cutting to make final biscuit. Place on parchment paper–lined rimmed baking sheet.

Brush tops with egg. Bake in 400°F (200°C) oven until golden, about 12 minutes. Transfer to rack; let cool.

MAKES 18 BISCUITS. PER BISCUIT: about 95 cal, 3 g pro, 4 g total fat (2 g sat. fat), 13 g carb, 1 g fibre, 18 mg chol, 167 mg sodium, 35 mg potassium. % RDI: 4% calcium, 6% iron, 3% vit A, 1% folate.

Soda bread is leavened with a combination of baking soda and buttermilk instead of yeast. Whole wheat flour makes this loaf a little denser than one made with just all-purpose flour, but the bread's chewy texture is satisfying and homey.

SIMPLE SODA BREAD

1 cup **all-purpose flour**

1 cup **whole wheat flour**

1 tbsp **granulated sugar**

2 tsp **baking powder**

½ tsp **baking soda**

¼ tsp **salt**

¼ cup **dried currants**

½ tsp **caraway seeds** (optional)

¾ cup **buttermilk**

3 tbsp **butter,** melted

1 **egg**

In large bowl, whisk together all-purpose flour, whole wheat flour, sugar, baking powder, baking soda and salt; stir in currants, and caraway seeds (if using).

Whisk together buttermilk, butter and egg; pour over flour mixture, tossing with fork to form sticky dough.

Scrape onto floured surface; gently knead 10 times. Transfer to parchment paper–lined baking sheet; press into 7-inch (18 cm) round. With sharp knife, score top into 8 wedges.

Bake in 350°F (180°C) oven until cake tester inserted in centre comes out clean, about 35 minutes. Transfer to rack; let cool.

MAKES 6 TO 8 SERVINGS. PER EACH OF 8 SERVINGS: about 188 cal, 6 g pro, 6 g total fat (4 g sat. fat), 30 g carb, 3 g fibre, 37 mg chol, 286 mg sodium, 171 mg potassium. % RDI: 8% calcium, 12% iron, 5% vit A, 1% vit C, 19% folate.

Soda breads are so simple to make, and they taste just as wonderful as yeast breads. Their rustic texture and appearance make them lovely companions for a cheese plate or for homemade soups or stews.

WHOLE SPELT SODA BREAD

2½ cups **whole spelt flour** (approx)

2 tbsp **granulated sugar**

1¼ tsp **baking soda**

½ tsp **salt**

2 tbsp cold **butter,** cubed

1 **egg white**

⅔ cup **buttermilk**

In large bowl, whisk together spelt flour, sugar, baking soda and salt. Using pastry blender or 2 knives, cut in butter until in coarse crumbs.

Whisk egg white with buttermilk; with fork, stir into flour mixture to form soft dough.

Turn out onto lightly floured surface; with floured hands, press dough into ball. Knead gently 10 times. Place on greased baking sheet; gently pat out into 6-inch (15 cm) round. Dust top lightly with spelt flour; with serrated knife, score top with large X.

Bake in 375°F (190°C) oven until lightly browned and cake tester inserted in centre comes out clean, 35 to 40 minutes. Transfer to rack; let cool.

MAKES 6 TO 8 SERVINGS. PER EACH OF 8 SERVINGS: about 175 cal, 6 g pro, 4 g total fat (2 g sat. fat), 31 g carb, 5 g fibre, 10 mg chol, 385 mg sodium. % RDI: 3% calcium, 11% iron, 3% vit A, 5% folate.

Some white-flour dinner rolls can be pillowy and not terribly substantial. But this simple, wheaty dough bakes into tender, buttery buns that offer a bit more fibre, a more pleasing texture and a richer, more satisfying flavour. Make a variety of the shapes on pages 58 and 59 for entertaining during the holidays.

WHOLE WHEAT SOFT DINNER ROLL DOUGH

2 tbsp **granulated sugar**

1¼ cups **milk**

¼ cup **butter**

1 tsp **salt**

¼ cup warm **water**

1 pkg (8 g) **active dry yeast** (2¼ tsp)

1 **egg**

3 cups **all-purpose flour** (approx)

1½ cups **whole wheat flour**

Remove 1 tsp of the sugar; set aside.

In saucepan, heat together milk, butter, salt and remaining sugar until butter is melted; let cool to lukewarm.

In large bowl, dissolve reserved sugar in warm water. Sprinkle in yeast; let stand until frothy, about 10 minutes.

Whisk in milk mixture and egg. Stir in 2½ cups of the all-purpose flour and whole wheat flour, 1 cup at a time, to make soft shaggy dough.

Turn out onto lightly floured surface; knead, adding as much of the remaining all-purpose flour as necessary to prevent sticking, until smooth, elastic and quite soft, about 10 minutes.

Place dough in greased large bowl; turn to grease all over. Cover and let rise in warm draft-free place until doubled in bulk, about 1½ hours. Shape and bake as desired (see pages 58 and 59).

MAKES ABOUT 2¼ LB (1.015 KG) DOUGH, OR ENOUGH FOR ABOUT 20 ROLLS.

From left: Cloverleaf, Topknot,
Fantan and Knot Dinner Rolls
(pages 58 and 59)

These pretty little overhand knots are fun to make and look like they are fresh from the bakery.

KNOT DINNER ROLLS

Whole Wheat Soft Dinner Roll Dough (page 55)
1 egg yolk

Punch down dough. Turn out onto lightly floured surface; divide into 20 pieces.

Roll each piece into 9-inch (23 cm) rope; tie each in knot. Place rolls, 2 inches (5 cm) apart, on parchment paper–lined baking sheets. Cover and let rise in warm draft-free place until doubled in bulk, about 1 hour.

Whisk egg yolk with 2 tsp water; brush over rolls. Bake in 375°F (190°C) oven until golden and rolls sound hollow when tapped on bottoms, 22 to 25 minutes.

Let cool on pans on racks for 10 minutes. Transfer to racks and let cool.

MAKES 20 ROLLS. PER ROLL: about 143 cal, 4 g pro, 3 g total fat (2 g sat. fat), 24 g carb, 1 g fibre, 27 mg chol, 142 mg sodium, 66 mg potassium. % RDI: 2% calcium, 10% iron, 4% vit A, 32% folate.

These rolls look fancy, but shaping them couldn't be easier: The three little balls of dough used for each roll rise and meld into a delicious cloverleaf shape.

CLOVERLEAF DINNER ROLLS

Whole Wheat Soft Dinner Roll Dough (page 55)
1 egg yolk

Punch down dough. Turn out onto lightly floured surface; divide into 20 pieces. Divide each into 3 pieces; shape each into ball, stretching and pinching dough underneath to make tops smooth.

Place 3 balls in each of 20 greased muffin cups. Cover and let rise in warm draft-free place until doubled in bulk, about 1 hour.

Whisk egg yolk with 2 tsp water; brush over rolls. Bake in 375°F (190°C) oven until golden and rolls sound hollow when tapped on bottoms, about 25 minutes.

Let cool in pans on racks for 10 minutes. Transfer to racks and let cool.

MAKE 20 ROLLS. PER ROLL: about 143 cal, 4 g pro, 3 g total fat (2 g sat. fat), 24 g carb, 1 g fibre, 27 mg chol, 142 mg sodium, 66 mg potassium. % RDI: 2% calcium, 10% iron, 4% vit A, 32% folate.

As they bake, the buttery layers of these whole wheat rolls fan out so you can pull them apart at the table.

FANTAN DINNER ROLLS

Whole Wheat Soft Dinner Roll
   Dough (page 55)
2 tbsp **butter,** softened
1 egg yolk

Punch down dough; divide in half. On lightly floured surface, roll 1 half out into 16- x 10-inch (40 x 25 cm) rectangle. Brush with half of the butter. Cut into forty 2-inch (5 cm) squares. Place, butter side up, in 10 stacks of 4 squares each. Place stacks, on sides, in 10 greased muffin cups, fanning out layers. Repeat with remaining dough.

Cover and let rise in warm draft-free place until doubled in bulk, about 1 hour.

Whisk egg yolk with 2 tsp water; brush over rolls. Bake in 375°F (190°C) oven until golden and rolls sound hollow when tapped on bottoms, 22 to 25 minutes.

Let cool in pans on racks for 10 minutes. Transfer to racks and let cool.

MAKES 20 ROLLS. PER ROLL: about 153 cal, 4 g pro, 5 g total fat (3 g sat. fat), 24 g carb, 1 g fibre, 30 mg chol, 150 mg sodium, 66 mg potassium. % RDI: 2% calcium, 10% iron, 5% vit A, 32% folate.

Shaped like pretty little French brioches, these rolls look impressive, but shaping them is totally straightforward.

TOPKNOT DINNER ROLLS

Whole Wheat Soft Dinner Roll
   Dough (page 55)
1 egg yolk

Punch down dough. Turn out onto lightly floured surface; divide into 20 pieces. Remove 1 tsp from each piece; shape into ball and set aside.

Shape remaining pieces of dough into balls, stretching and pinching dough underneath to make tops smooth. Place each in greased muffin cup; gently press small ball on centre of each. Cover and let rise in warm draft-free place until doubled in bulk, about 1 hour.

Whisk egg yolk with 2 tsp water; brush over rolls. Bake in 375°F (190°C) oven until golden and rolls sound hollow when tapped on bottoms, 22 to 25 minutes.

Let cool in pans on racks for 10 minutes. Transfer to racks and let cool.

MAKES 20 ROLLS. PER ROLL: about 143 cal, 4 g pro, 3 g total fat (2 g sat. fat), 24 g carb, 1 g fibre, 27 mg chol, 142 mg sodium, 66 mg potassium. % RDI: 2% calcium, 10% iron, 4% vit A, 32% folate.

This loaf, with its lovely wheaty flavour, even crumb and rustic artisanal look, will make even novices into confirmed bread bakers. You have to begin the day before, mixing the starter, but this loaf is worth it. For this and the whole wheat variation, we used Robin Hood Best for Bread flours.

100% MULTIGRAIN LOAF

4 cups **multigrain bread flour** (approx)

1 cup warm **water**

2 tbsp **buckwheat honey**

1½ tsp **fine sea salt**

STARTER:

1 tsp **granulated sugar**

1 cup warm **water**

1½ tsp **active dry yeast**

1 cup **multigrain bread flour**

TOPPING:

½ tsp **multigrain bread flour**

STARTER: In bowl, dissolve sugar in warm water. Sprinkle in yeast; let stand until frothy, 10 minutes. Stir in flour until mixture is like thick pancake batter, 2 minutes. Cover with plastic wrap; let stand in warm place until puffy and a wheaty aroma develops, 8 to 12 hours.

Stir in 3¼ cups of the flour, warm water, honey and salt to make soft sticky dough. Turn out onto well-floured surface; knead, adding remaining flour as needed, until smooth and elastic, 8 minutes. Form into ball. Place in greased bowl; turn to grease all over. Cover; let rise in warm place until doubled in bulk, 1 to 1½ hours.

Punch down dough; shape into ball. Cover and let rest for 10 minutes. Press into 11- x 8-inch (28 x 20 cm) rectangle.

Starting at 1 short edge, roll up into cylinder; pinch seam and ends to seal. Fit, seam side down, into greased 9- x 5-inch (2 L) loaf pan. Cover and let rise in warm place until doubled in bulk, 1 to 1½ hours.

TOPPING: Dust top of loaf with flour. Slash top lengthwise down centre, starting and ending 1 inch (2.5 cm) from edges.

Bake in 375°F (190°C) oven until instant-read thermometer inserted in centre registers 215°F (101°C) and loaf is golden and sounds hollow when tapped on bottom, 50 to 60 minutes. Transfer to rack; let cool.

CHANGE IT UP

100% Whole Wheat Loaf

Replace multigrain bread flour with whole wheat bread flour.

MAKES 1 LOAF, OR 12 SLICES. PER SLICE: about 219 cal, 8 g pro, 1 g total fat (trace sat. fat) 45 g carb, 4 g fibre, 0 mg chol, 290 mg sodium. % RDI: 2% calcium, 19% iron, 2% vit C, 11% folate.

Roasting the garlic brings out its mild flavour and natural sweetness, so don't be afraid of using the whole head in this loaf. Serve slices of the bread with your favourite antipasti.

ROASTED GARLIC & SUN-DRIED TOMATO LOAF

1 head **garlic**

3 tbsp **extra-virgin olive oil**

½ tsp **granulated sugar**

1 cup warm **water**

1 pkg (8 g) **active dry yeast** (2¼ tsp)

2 tbsp finely chopped drained **oil-packed sun-dried tomatoes**

1 tsp **salt**

2 cups **white bread flour** (approx)

1 cup **multigrain bread flour** or whole wheat bread flour

Slice top off garlic to expose cloves. Place garlic on foil; drizzle with 1 tbsp of the oil. Wrap and bake in 375°F (190°C) oven until garlic cloves are soft, 45 to 60 minutes. Let cool. Squeeze cloves into small bowl and mash. Set aside.

In large bowl, dissolve sugar in warm water. Sprinkle in yeast; let stand until frothy, about 10 minutes. Stir in remaining oil, tomatoes, salt and mashed garlic. Stir in 1¾ cups of the white bread flour and multigrain flour to make sticky dough.

Turn out onto lightly floured surface; knead, adding as much of the remaining white flour as necessary to prevent sticking, until smooth and elastic, about 8 minutes.

Place in greased bowl; turn to grease all over. Cover and let rise in warm draft-free place until doubled in bulk, 1 to 1½ hours.

Punch down dough; turn out onto lightly floured surface. Pat into 11-inch (28 cm) circle. Roll up into cylinder with tapered ends. Pinch seam to smooth and seal. Place on parchment paper–lined baking sheet. Cover and let rise until doubled in bulk, 1¼ to 1½ hours.

With sharp knife, cut 4 shallow slashes diagonally across top of loaf. Bake in 375°F (190°C) oven until loaf sounds hollow when tapped on bottom, about 40 minutes. Transfer to rack; let cool.

MAKES 1 LOAF, OR 12 SLICES. PER SLICE: about 163 cal, 5 g pro, 4 g total fat (1 g sat. fat), 26 g carb, 2 g fibre, 0 mg chol, 197 mg sodium. % RDI: 1% calcium, 12% iron, 3% vit C, 19% folate.

Honey and milk give this loaf its subtle sweetness and soft crumb. If you prefer free-form loaves, shape each cylinder of the rolled-up dough into an oval, stretching and pinching the dough underneath to smooth the top. Place the loaves on a greased baking sheet instead of in loaf pans.

WHOLE WHEAT HONEY OAT LOAF

1 cup **boiling water**

1 cup **large-flake rolled oats**

¼ cup **liquid honey**

2 tbsp **butter,** melted

1 pkg (8 g) **active dry yeast** (2¼ tsp)

1 cup warm **homogenized milk**

2 cups **whole wheat flour**

2 cups **all-purpose flour** (approx)

2 tsp **salt**

TOPPING:

1 **egg,** beaten

1 tbsp **large-flake rolled oats**

In heatproof bowl, pour boiling water over oats; let stand until water is absorbed, 15 minutes. Stir in honey and butter.

Meanwhile, in large bowl, sprinkle yeast over milk; let stand until frothy, about 10 minutes. Stir in oat mixture. Stir in whole wheat flour, 1 cup of the all-purpose flour and salt to form sticky dough.

Turn out onto floured surface; knead, adding remaining all-purpose flour as necessary to prevent sticking, until smooth and elastic, 12 minutes. Place in greased bowl; turn to grease all over. Cover and let rise in warm draft-free place until doubled in bulk, 1 to 1½ hours.

Punch down dough; divide in half. On floured surface, pat each into 11- x 8-inch (28 x 20 cm) rectangle.

Starting at narrow end, roll up into cylinders; pinch seams and ends to seal. Fit, seam side down, into 2 parchment paper–lined 8- x 4-inch (1.5 L) loaf pans. Cover; let rise in warm place until doubled, 1 hour.

TOPPING: Brush loaves with egg; sprinkle with oats. Bake in 375°F (190°C) oven until loaves sound hollow when tapped on bottoms, 40 to 50 minutes. Transfer to racks; let cool.

CHANGE IT UP

Whole Wheat Honey Oatmeal Rolls
Shape punched-down dough into 18 balls, pinching underneath to smooth tops. Place, 2 inches (5 cm) apart, on parchment paper–lined baking sheet. Cover; let rise for 1 hour. Reduce baking time to 30 to 35 minutes.
MAKES 18 ROLLS.

MAKES 2 LOAVES, 12 SLICES EACH. PER SLICE: about 117 cal, 4 g pro, 2 g total fat (1 g sat. fat), 22 g carb, 2 g fibre, 12 mg chol, 207 mg sodium, 93 mg potassium. % RDI: 2% calcium, 9% iron, 1% vit A, 15% folate.

This rustic baguette-style bread, called *pain aux noix* in France, is delicious toasted. The French use a soupy fermented starter called a *poolish* – made of flour, yeast and water – to develop the bread's distinctive tangy character.

HAZELNUT HONEY BREAD

1½ cups sliced **hazelnuts**

¾ tsp **active dry yeast**

½ cup warm **water**

2½ cups **all-purpose flour** (approx)

1 cup **whole wheat flour**

½ cup **milk**

⅓ cup **liquid honey**

2 tbsp **butter,** melted

2 tsp **salt**

STARTER:

¾ tsp **active dry yeast**

½ cup warm **water**

¾ cup **all-purpose flour**

TIP: For an artisan-style crust, place loaves in oven, then spritz walls and floor with cold water (avoiding lightbulb) until steam fills oven, about 10 seconds. Quickly close oven door to trap steam; wait for 5 minutes, then repeat steaming.

STARTER: In bowl, sprinkle yeast over warm water; let stand for 1 minute. Stir until dissolved. Add flour; stir until same consistency as pancake batter, 2 minutes. Cover with plastic wrap; place in warm draft-free place until bubbly and doubled in bulk, 4 hours.

In food processor, finely chop half of the hazelnuts; set aside.

In large bowl, sprinkle yeast over warm water; let stand for 1 minute. Stir until dissolved. Stir starter; add to yeast mixture. Add 2 cups of the all-purpose flour, whole wheat flour, sliced and chopped hazelnuts, milk, ¼ cup of the honey, butter and salt; stir until soft ragged dough forms. Turn out onto floured surface; knead, adding remaining all-purpose flour as needed, until smooth and elastic, 10 minutes.

Place in greased bowl; turn to grease all over. Cover; let rise in warm draft-free place until doubled in bulk, 1½ to 2 hours. Punch down dough; knead into ball. Divide in half; shape each into ball. Pull each into 11- x 8-inch (28 x 20 cm) rectangle, with 1 long side facing you. Starting at bottom right corner, diagonally roll up each into cylinder; pinch seams and ends to seal. Place, seam side down and at least 3 inches (8 cm) apart, on parchment paper–lined large rimless baking sheet. Cut 3 diagonal slashes in top of each. Cover and let rise until doubled in bulk, about 1 hour.

Stir remaining honey with 1 tbsp warm water; brush over loaves. Bake in 400°F (200°C) oven until loaves sound hollow when tapped on bottoms, 25 to 30 minutes. Transfer to rack; let cool.

MAKES 2 LOAVES, 16 SLICES EACH. PER SLICE: about 112 cal, 3 g pro, 4 g total fat (1 g sat. fat), 16 g carb, 1 g fibre, 3 mg chol, 153 mg sodium. % RDI: 1% calcium, 7% iron, 1% vit A, 12% folate.

This soda-leavened bread makes a dense, slightly crumbly loaf with a rich, nutty flavour. Slather it with Smoked Mackerel Pâté (opposite) or top with butter, smoked salmon and a sprinkle of chives.

IRISH BROWN BREAD

1 cup **all-purpose flour** (approx)

1 cup **whole wheat flour**

½ cup **quick-cooking rolled oats** (not instant)

¼ cup **natural raw wheat germ**

1½ tsp **baking soda**

1½ tsp **caraway seeds**

½ tsp **salt**

½ cup cold **butter,** cubed

1 cup **buttermilk**

2 tbsp **cooking molasses** or fancy molasses

In large bowl, whisk together all-purpose and whole wheat flours, oats, wheat germ, baking soda, caraway seeds and salt. With pastry blender or 2 knives, cut in butter until in fine crumbs. Whisk buttermilk with molasses; stir into flour mixture to make soft dough.

Turn out onto lightly floured surface; knead gently about 10 times. Shape into 8-inch (20 cm) long oval; dust top lightly with all-purpose flour. With serrated knife, cut shallow slash lengthwise down centre; transfer to greased 9- x 5-inch (2 L) loaf pan.

Bake in 375°F (190°C) oven until loaf sounds hollow when tapped on bottom, about 45 minutes.

Let cool in pan on rack for 5 minutes. Transfer to rack; let cool completely. (Make-ahead: Store in airtight container for up to 4 days. Or wrap in plastic wrap and freeze in airtight container for up to 2 weeks.)

MAKES 1 LOAF, OR 12 SLICES. PER SLICE: about 183 cal, 4 g pro, 9 g total fat (5 g sat. fat), 23 g carb, 2 g fibre, 21 mg chol, 332 mg sodium. % RDI: 4% calcium, 10% iron, 7% vit A, 14% folate.

Mackerel was once regarded as poor man's trout, but these days it's appreciated for its gutsy, robust flavour. If you like, garnish this pâté with more chopped fresh parsley or green onion.

SMOKED MACKEREL PÂTÉ

12 oz (340 g) **smoked mackerel** (about 3 fillets)

½ cup **fresh bread crumbs**

⅓ cup **whipping cream** (35%)

¼ cup **butter,** softened

1 tbsp **lemon juice**

Pinch **cayenne pepper**

2 tbsp finely chopped **fresh parsley**

2 tbsp finely chopped **green onion**

Skin and bone mackerel. In food processor, pulse together mackerel, bread crumbs, cream, butter, lemon juice and cayenne pepper just until puréed.

Stir in parsley and green onion. *(Make-ahead: Refrigerate in airtight container for up to 5 days. Let come to room temperature before serving.)*

MAKES ABOUT 2 CUPS. PER 1 TBSP: about 46 cal, 3 g pro, 4 g total fat (2 g sat. fat), 1 g carb, 0 g fibre, 17 mg chol, 95 mg sodium. % RDI: 1% calcium, 1% iron, 2% vit A, 2% vit C, 1% folate.

This dough is moist and needs a long kneading (which is easiest to do in a stand mixer) and an overnight rise in the refrigerator to create an airy yet chewy texture. Whole spelt flour gives this focaccia a subtle nut-like flavour; you can replace it with whole wheat flour, if you prefer. Serve warm or at room temperature.

WHOLE GRAIN CHEDDAR CHIPOTLE FOCACCIA

¾ tsp **active dry yeast**

Pinch **ground cumin**

1¼ cups warm **water**

1¾ cups **whole wheat flour** (approx)

1¾ cups **whole spelt flour**

3 tbsp **olive oil**

1½ tsp **salt**

2 **dried chipotle peppers**

Boiling water

½ tsp crumbled **dried oregano**

1 cup shredded **extra-old Cheddar cheese** or up to 3-year-old Cheddar cheese

✱ TIPS:

- To prevent the dough from taking on any fridge odours during its overnight stay, place the covered bowl in a plastic bag.
- To skip the soaking step, you can substitute drained canned chipotle peppers in adobo sauce for the dried chipotles. Seed and chop as directed.

In bowl of stand mixer (or large bowl), sprinkle yeast and cumin over warm water; let stand until frothy, about 10 minutes. Mix in whole wheat flour, spelt flour, oil and salt. Using dough hook, knead at medium-low speed for 5 minutes. Continue kneading, adding a little more whole wheat flour, 1 tbsp at a time, as needed to prevent sticking, until dough barely holds together and is still slightly sticky but smooth, 7 to 10 minutes. (Or knead with wooden spoon, then oiled hands, for 20 minutes.) Transfer to greased bowl; turn to grease all over. Cover with plastic wrap; refrigerate overnight.

Bring to room temperature, 2 to 3 hours. Meanwhile, soak chipotle peppers in boiling water until softened, 15 minutes. Drain, stem, seed and chop peppers.

Lightly push down dough. Turn out onto floured surface; knead in peppers. Shape into ball, stretching and pinching dough underneath to smooth top. Place on floured rimless baking sheet; cover and let rise in warm draft-free place until doubled in bulk, 1 hour.

On floured parchment paper, press and pull dough, letting rest if too elastic, into 16- x 12-inch (40 x 30 cm) rectangle. Slide paper and dough onto baking sheet. Cover; let rise until puffed, 30 minutes.

With fingertips, press indentations into dough; sprinkle with oregano, then cheese. Place in 425°F (220°C) oven. Spritz walls and floor with cold water (avoiding lightbulb) until steam fills oven; close door to trap steam. Bake until bottom is golden, 15 to 18 minutes.

MAKES 1 LOAF, OR 12 TO 16 PIECES. PER EACH OF 16 PIECES: about 97 cal, 4 g pro, 5 g total fat (2 g sat. fat), 10 g carb, 2 g fibre, 7 mg chol, 271 mg sodium, 65 mg potassium. % RDI: 5% calcium, 4% iron, 3% vit A, 5% folate.

Red Fife wheat is a heritage grain that is regaining popularity across Canada. Here, it is combined with walnuts and honey in a sweet quick bread that's nice paired with aged cheeses or just a cup of tea. Look for Red Fife flour in specialty or organic food stores. If you can't find it, substitute stone-ground whole wheat flour.

HONEY WALNUT RED FIFE WHEAT LOAF

1 cup chopped **walnuts**

1½ cups **all-purpose flour**

¾ cup **stone-ground Red Fife flour**

1 tsp **baking powder**

½ tsp **baking soda**

½ tsp **salt**

⅔ cup **buttermilk**

½ cup **unsalted butter,** melted

½ cup **flavourful liquid honey**
 (such as buckwheat honey)

¼ cup **granulated sugar**

2 **eggs**

TOPPING:
2 tbsp chopped **walnuts**

GLAZE:
3 tbsp **flavourful liquid honey**
 (such as buckwheat honey)

1 tbsp **water**

Toast walnuts on baking sheet in 325°F (160°C) oven until golden and fragrant, 7 to 8 minutes. Let cool.

In large bowl, stir together all-purpose and Red Fife flours, baking powder, baking soda and salt. Whisk together buttermilk, butter, honey, sugar and eggs. Pour over flour mixture; sprinkle with toasted walnuts. Stir just until moistened.

TOPPING: Scrape batter into parchment paper–lined 8- x 4-inch (1.5 L) loaf pan; sprinkle with walnuts. Bake in 325°F (160°C) oven until cake tester inserted in centre comes out clean, 1 hour.

GLAZE: In glass measure, microwave honey and water at high until boiling, about 1 minute. Poke top of hot loaf all over with skewer; brush with glaze. Let cool in pan on rack for 10 minutes. Transfer to rack; let cool completely. (*Make-ahead: Wrap and store at room temperature for up to 2 days, or overwrap in foil and freeze for up to 2 weeks.*)

MAKES 1 LOAF, OR 12 SLICES. PER SLICE: about 323 cal, 6 g pro, 16 g total fat (6 g sat. fat), 41 g carb, 2 g fibre, 52 mg chol, 198 mg sodium, 122 mg potassium. % RDI: 5% calcium, 11% iron, 8% vit A, 26% folate.

In Switzerland, mixed-grain breads are usually half white flour and half differing amounts of rye, whole wheat and spelt. They have a rich flavour and a texture midway between light, airy French or Italian loaves and dense German loaves. This bread uses a *levain*, a French sourdough starter, and requires two separate overnight risings. But it's worth the time.

MIXED-GRAIN SWISS COUNTRY LOAF

⅔ cup warm **water**

1 tbsp **barley malt syrup** or wheat malt syrup

½ tsp **active dry yeast**

½ cup **whole spelt flour**

2 tsp **salt**

2¼ cups **white bread flour** (approx)

LEVAIN:

1 cup + 2 tbsp warm **water**

1 tsp **milk**

½ tsp **active dry yeast**

⅔ cup **dark rye flour**

⅔ cup **white bread flour**

⅓ cup **whole wheat flour**

LEVAIN: In large bowl, stir warm water with milk. Sprinkle yeast over top; let stand until frothy, about 10 minutes.

Stir in rye flour, white bread flour and whole wheat flour until smooth. With wooden spoon, beat 100 strokes in same direction until gluey. Scrape down side of bowl. Cover with plastic wrap; let stand at cool room temperature in draft-free place for 12 to 24 hours.

In bowl of stand mixer, stir warm water with malt syrup. Sprinkle in yeast; let stand until frothy, about 10 minutes.

Stir in spelt flour and salt. Scrape in levain; beat until combined. Stir in white bread flour to form wet shaggy dough.

Using dough hook on medium-low speed, knead, adding up to ½ cup more white bread flour as needed to prevent sticking, until smooth and elastic, 12 to 15 minutes.

Transfer to greased bowl; turn to grease all over. Cover with plastic wrap; refrigerate overnight.

Bring to room temperature, 2 to 3 hours. Lightly push down dough; knead lightly for 1 minute. Shape into ball, stretching and pinching dough underneath to smooth top. Cover and let rest for 15 minutes.

Press dough into 12- x 8-inch (30 x 20 cm) rectangle; fold long sides to centre, pinching together seam and ends. Cut 20-inch (50 cm) length of thin kitchen string and lay across centre of parchment paper–lined baking sheet. Place loaf, seam side down, on string, with string crosswise under centre and both ends exposed. Cover and let rise in warm draft-free place until doubled in bulk, about 1 hour.

Score ½-inch (1 cm) deep slash lengthwise down centre of loaf; bring ends of string to centre, cutting through centre of loaf. Remove string.

Place in 450°F (230°C) oven. Spritz walls and floor with cold water (avoiding lightbulb) until steam fills oven; close door to trap steam. Bake for 20 minutes, repeating steaming after 3 minutes.

Reduce heat to 400°F (200°C); bake until crust is hard, loaf sounds hollow when tapped on bottom and instant-read thermometer inserted in centre registers 200°F (93°C), about 20 minutes. Transfer to rack; let cool.

TIP: If you don't have or don't want to use a stand mixer, mix the ingredients in a large bowl, then turn out dough onto floured surface and knead by hand for about 20 minutes.

MAKES 1 LARGE LOAF, OR 20 SLICES. PER SLICE: about 109 cal, 4 g pro, 1 g total fat (trace sat. fat), 22 g carb, 2 g fibre, 0 mg chol, 231 mg sodium, 67 mg potassium. % RDI: 1% calcium, 9% iron, 13% folate.

Inspired by the famous cinnamon buns of Winnipeg's Tall Grass Prairie Bread Company, which features local grains and ingredients in its many offerings, these buns are a bit more virtuous than the white-flour version. If you like them glazed, mix 1¼ cups icing sugar with 2 tbsp milk and drizzle over top while still hot.

WHOLE WHEAT CINNAMON BUNS

¼ cup **granulated sugar**

⅓ cup warm **water**

1½ tsp **active dry yeast**

⅔ cup **milk**

1 **egg**

2 tbsp **butter,** melted and cooled

½ tsp **vanilla**

1¾ cups **all-purpose flour** (approx)

1⅓ cups **whole wheat flour**

½ tsp **salt**

FILLING:

1 cup packed **brown sugar**

1½ tsp **cinnamon**

Pinch each **ground cloves** and **salt**

⅓ cup **butter,** melted

In bowl, dissolve 1 tsp of the sugar in warm water. Sprinkle in yeast; let stand until frothy, about 10 minutes.

In separate bowl, whisk milk, egg, butter, vanilla and remaining sugar; stir in yeast mixture.

In large bowl, whisk all-purpose flour, whole wheat flour and salt; stir in milk mixture until ragged dough forms. Turn out onto floured surface; knead, adding up to 2 tbsp more all-purpose flour if needed, until soft, smooth but not sticky dough forms, about 10 minutes.

Transfer to greased bowl; turn to grease all over. Cover and let rise in warm draft-free place until doubled in bulk, about 2 hours.

FILLING: Meanwhile, stir together brown sugar, cinnamon, cloves and salt; set aside. Turn dough out onto floured surface; roll out into 20- x 12-inch (50 x 30 cm) rectangle. Leaving ½-inch (1 cm) border uncovered at 1 long edge, brush with all but 2 tbsp of the butter. Leaving same border uncovered, sprinkle with sugar mixture. Starting at edge opposite border, tightly roll up; pinch seam to seal. Brush with remaining butter.

With sharp knife, cut into 12 pieces; place, cut side up, in greased 13- x 9-inch (3 L) baking dish. Cover; let rise in warm place until doubled in bulk, 1 hour. (*Make-ahead: Cover; refrigerate for up to 12 hours. Let stand at room temperature for 30 minutes before baking.*)

Bake in 375°F (190°C) oven until tops are golden and buns sound hollow when gently tapped, 25 to 30 minutes. Serve warm.

MAKES 12 BUNS. PER BUN: about 274 cal, 5 g pro, 8 g total fat (5 g sat. fat), 47 g carb, 3 g fibre, 35 mg chol, 165 mg sodium, 176 mg potassium. % RDI: 4% calcium, 14% iron, 7% vit A, 25% folate.

Moist, delicious and quick to prepare, this cake is great for snacking or for a special breakfast treat. Try it with a dollop of rich Blueberry Sauce (opposite) for a scrumptious dessert.

BLUEBERRY RASPBERRY SPELT CAKE

1½ cups **fresh raspberries**

1 cup **fresh blueberries**

¾ cup **all-purpose flour**

1½ cups **whole spelt flour**

½ tsp each **baking powder** and **baking soda**

¼ tsp **salt**

3 **eggs**

⅔ cup **granulated sugar**

⅓ cup **butter,** melted

¼ cup **vegetable oil**

1 tsp **vanilla**

⅓ cup **sliced almonds** (optional)

Line bottom of 8-inch (2 L) square cake pan with parchment paper; grease sides. Set aside.

Toss together raspberries, blueberries and 2 tbsp of the all-purpose flour; set aside.

Whisk together spelt flour, remaining all-purpose flour, baking powder, baking soda and salt.

In large bowl, beat eggs with sugar until pale and thickened, about 3 minutes. Stir in butter, oil and vanilla. Stir in flour mixture until smooth; fold in berry mixture. Scrape into prepared pan; sprinkle with almonds (if using).

Bake in 325°F (160°C) oven until golden and cake tester inserted in centre comes out clean, about 50 minutes.

Let cool in pan on rack. (*Make-ahead: Cover and store at room temperature for up to 2 days. Or wrap in plastic wrap and freeze in airtight container for up to 2 weeks.*)

MAKES 8 TO 12 SERVINGS. PER EACH OF 12 SERVINGS: about 250 cal, 5 g pro, 12 g total fat (4 g sat. fat), 32 g carb, 3 g fibre, 60 mg chol, 166 mg sodium. % RDI: 2% calcium, 4% iron, 6% vit A, 7% vit C, 11% folate.

When blueberries are in season, make this sauce often to serve with cakes, waffles and pancakes. In the winter, try it with thawed frozen blueberries.

BLUEBERRY SAUCE

2 cups **blueberries**

¼ cup **granulated sugar**

½ tsp grated **lemon zest**

3 tbsp **lemon juice**

2 tsp **all-purpose flour**

In saucepan, combine blueberries, sugar, lemon zest and lemon juice. Whisk flour with 2 tbsp water; add to saucepan and bring to boil over medium heat.

Reduce heat and simmer, stirring often, until thickened and blueberries have broken down, about 6 minutes. *(Make-ahead: Refrigerate in airtight container for up to 2 days; rewarm to serve, adding about 1 tbsp water to thin if necessary.)*

MAKES ABOUT 1½ CUPS. PER 1 TBSP: about 16 cal, trace pro, 0 g total fat (0 g sat. fat), 4 g carb, trace fibre, 0 mg chol, 0 mg sodium, 12 mg potassium. % RDI: 2% vit C.

BROWN RICE & WILD RICE

Mixed grains make for interesting porridge. Look for brands such as Bob's Red Mill in the natural food section of your supermarket; their 10-grain mix contains wheat, rye, triticale, oat bran, oats, corn, barley, brown rice, millet and flaxseeds. Toasting the grains before baking them in this creamy breakfast adds a deep, nutty flavour.

MAPLE-BAKED GRAINS WITH BANANAS & PECANS

1½ cups **10-grain hot cereal**

2 cups **milk**

¼ cup **maple syrup**

¼ tsp **salt**

2 **bananas,** sliced

½ cup chopped **pecans,** toasted

In skillet, toast cereal over medium heat, stirring often, until light golden, about 7 minutes. Transfer to bowl.

Stir in milk, 1½ cups water, maple syrup and salt. Scrape into greased 8-inch (2 L) square baking dish.

Bake in 400°F (200°C) oven until liquid is absorbed and grains are softened, about 45 minutes. Serve topped with bananas and pecans.

TIP: This breakfast is a nice background for other tasty flavour combinations. You can substitute your favourite fruits and nuts for the bananas and pecans if you like. Try apples with walnuts, or berries with almonds.

MAKES 4 SERVINGS. PER SERVING: about 470 cal, 15 g pro, 14 g total fat (2 g sat. fat), 77 g carb, 10 g fibre, 10 mg chol, 205 mg sodium. % RDI: 16% calcium, 6% iron, 6% vit A, 8% vit C, 8% folate.

This rich vegetarian main dish has a woodsy flavour, courtesy of a delicious mixture of regular and exotic mushrooms. Serve the torte with a green salad for a simple bistro-style meal at home.

MUSHROOM BROWN RICE TORTE

1 cup **brown rice**

2 tbsp **olive oil**

1 **onion,** thinly sliced

1¼ lb (565 g) **mixed mushrooms** (such as cremini, white or oyster mushrooms, or shiitake caps), trimmed and sliced

1 tsp chopped **fresh thyme**

1 tsp **salt**

½ tsp **pepper**

6 **eggs**

3 cups shredded **Fontina cheese** or old Cheddar cheese

¾ cup **10% cream** or milk

Line bottom and side of 10-inch (3 L) springform pan with parchment paper. Centre pan on large square of foil; press foil up side of pan.

Bring pot of salted water to boil over high heat; stir in rice. Reduce heat and simmer until tender, about 40 minutes. Drain in fine sieve; let cool completely in sieve.

Meanwhile, in large skillet, heat oil over medium-high heat; sauté onion until softened, about 4 minutes. Add mushrooms, thyme, and half each of the salt and pepper; sauté until mushrooms are softened and no liquid remains, 8 to 10 minutes.

In large bowl, beat 1 of the eggs; stir in rice. Pat evenly into bottom of prepared pan. Sprinkle with half of the cheese; spread mushroom mixture evenly over top.

Beat together remaining eggs, cream and remaining salt and pepper; pour evenly over top. Bake in 400°F (200°C) oven for 45 minutes. Sprinkle with remaining cheese; bake until bubbly and golden, about 15 minutes.

Let stand for 15 minutes before cutting into wedges.

MAKES 8 SERVINGS. PER SERVING: about 372 cal, 20 g pro, 22 g total fat (11 g sat. fat), 24 g carb, 3 g fibre, 192 mg chol, 977 mg sodium, 364 mg potassium. % RDI: 25% calcium, 11% iron, 18% vit A, 2% vit C, 16% folate.

Clockwise from top left: Parboiled long-grain brown rice, brown rice spaghetti, whole grain brown rice flour and short-grain brown rice

PROFILE:
BROWN RICE

WHY IT'S GOOD FOR YOU: Rice is a terrific pantry staple, and it's smart to use the whole grain form when you can. Brown rice is a tasty source of magnesium, phosphorus, B vitamins and fibre.

WHOLE GRAIN FORMS: Unrefined **brown rice** has just the husks removed, so it contains both the bran and the germ. Brown long-grain, short-grain and basmati rice are all widely available varieties. **Parboiled (converted) brown rice** is boiled or steamed under pressure, which seals in nutrients and creates a quicker-cooking, less-sticky version of brown rice. **Pasta** made from brown rice flour is a gluten-free option. It's a bit stickier than wheat pasta, so follow package directions closely.

Whole grain flour made from brown rice is used in many gluten-free baked goods. Because it doesn't contain gluten, it needs a boost from other flours or ingredients to give breads and cakes a proper rise.

STORAGE: Brown rice and brown rice flour contain oils that can go rancid, so store them in airtight containers in the refrigerator for up to six months, or in the freezer for up to a year. You can keep cooked brown rice in the fridge for up to two days. Brown rice pasta is fine on your pantry shelf.

USES: Brown rice has an earthy flavour and a chewy texture that might take getting used to, but you'll come to love it with stir-fries, in biryani or mixed with red beans and spices for a Caribbean twist. It can take up to twice as long to cook as white rice, so check the package directions.

From left: Brown Rice
Vegetable Maki Rolls and
Brown Rice Spicy Shrimp
Maki Rolls

Made with short-grain brown rice, these maki rolls are foolproof and contain more fibre than ones made with white rice. Keep a small bowl of water nearby and wet your fingers often to make spreading the rice easier. Serve the rolls with wasabi, pickled ginger and soy sauce for dipping.

BROWN RICE SPICY SHRIMP MAKI ROLLS

2 cups **short-grain brown rice**

⅓ cup **unseasoned rice vinegar**

4 tsp **granulated sugar**

1 tsp **salt**

6 sheets **roasted nori**

Half **English cucumber** (optional), peeled, seeded and julienned

SPICY SHRIMP FILLING:

1 lb (450 g) **frozen cooked peeled shrimp,** thawed and coarsely chopped

3 **green onions,** thinly sliced

⅓ cup **light mayonnaise**

2 tsp **sriracha** or other Asian chili paste

TIP: A bamboo sushi mat, or *makisu,* is inexpensive and makes rolling very easy. To keep it clean, wrap it in plastic wrap before using.

In saucepan, bring 4 cups water and rice to boil; reduce heat, cover and simmer until rice is tender and liquid is absorbed, about 50 minutes. Transfer to large shallow bowl; let cool for 10 minutes.

Meanwhile, in small saucepan, combine vinegar, sugar and salt; cook, stirring, over medium heat until sugar is dissolved, about 1 minute. Drizzle over rice; toss with wooden spoon to coat. Let cool to room temperature.

SPICY SHRIMP FILLING: Stir together shrimp, green onions, mayonnaise and sriracha.

Place sushi rolling mat on work surface with short side facing you; place 1 nori sheet, shiny side down, on mat. With wet fingers, press 1 cup of the rice evenly over nori, leaving 1-inch (2.5 cm) border on far side. Arrange ¼ cup of the shrimp mixture and one-sixth of the cucumber (if using) along closest edge.

Using mat as guide, roll up firmly, squeezing to compress. Repeat with remaining ingredients to make 6 rolls. With wet chef's knife, trim ends of each roll; cut each roll into eight ½-inch (1 cm) thick slices.

CHANGE IT UP
Brown Rice Vegetable Maki Rolls
Omit shrimp filling; fill rolls with thinly sliced avocado, and julienned sweet red pepper, daikon radish and cucumber.

MAKES 6 SERVINGS. PER SERVING: about 369 cal, 22 g pro, 7 g total fat (1 g sat. fat), 54 g carb, 4 g fibre, 152 mg chol, 670 mg sodium, 375 mg potassium. % RDI: 6% calcium, 27% iron, 13% vit A, 13% vit C, 18% folate.

Pork tenderloins are delicious rolled around a stuffing, and they make a nice low-cost main dish for entertaining. Serve with steamed fresh green beans and a spinach salad.

FRUIT & NUT–STUFFED PORK TENDERLOINS

2 **pork tenderloins** (12 oz/ 340 g each)

1 **egg**

¼ tsp **salt**

Pinch **pepper**

2 tsp **vegetable oil**

¾ cup **sodium-reduced beef broth**

½ cup **cranberry 100% juice blend**

2 tsp **cornstarch**

STUFFING:

1 tsp **vegetable oil**

1 **onion,** chopped

2 cloves **garlic,** minced

2 tsp crumbled **dried sage**

¼ cup **brown rice**

¼ cup **wild rice**

1 cup **sodium-reduced beef broth**

¼ cup **dried cranberries**

¼ cup chopped **pecans,** toasted

¼ tsp each **salt** and **pepper**

STUFFING: In saucepan, heat oil over medium heat; fry onion, garlic and sage, stirring often, until softened, about 5 minutes. Add brown rice and wild rice; stir to coat. Add broth and bring to boil; reduce heat, cover and simmer until rice is tender and liquid is absorbed, about 45 minutes. Add cranberries, pecans, salt and pepper; fluff with fork. Let cool.

Trim any fat from pork. Cut each tenderloin in half lengthwise almost but not all the way through; open like a book. Place between plastic wrap; pound each to generous ¼-inch (5 mm) thickness.

Mix egg into stuffing. Spoon half lengthwise down centre of each tenderloin. Roll up tenderloins around stuffing.

Tie tenderloins with kitchen string at 1-inch (2.5 cm) intervals. Sprinkle with salt and pepper.

In large ovenproof skillet, heat oil over medium-high heat; brown tenderloins. Transfer skillet to 375°F (190°C) oven; roast until just a hint of pink remains and juices run clear when pork is pierced, about 25 minutes. Transfer to cutting board and tent with foil; let stand for 10 minutes.

Meanwhile, drain off any fat from skillet. Add broth and cranberry juice; bring to boil, scraping up browned bits. Stir cornstarch with 1 tbsp water; whisk into skillet and boil, stirring, until thickened, about 1 minute. Cut pork diagonally into ½-inch (1 cm) thick slices. Serve with sauce.

MAKES 6 SERVINGS. PER SERVING: about 268 cal, 29 g pro, 8 g total fat (2 g sat. fat), 19 g carb, 2 g fibre, 94 mg chol, 446 mg sodium, 527 mg potassium. % RDI: 3% calcium, 14% iron, 2% vit A, 8% vit C, 9% folate.

Stuffing a whole trout can be messy. This recipe calls for skinless trout fillets layered with a flavourful wild rice filling – a simpler (but still beautiful) dish for a dinner party. Wow your guests by bringing it to the table whole and slicing it before their eyes. Look for identical-size sides of trout to create the proper sandwich look.

WILD RICE & SPINACH-STUFFED RAINBOW TROUT

¾ cup **wild rice**

1 tbsp **butter**

1 tbsp **olive oil**

3 **shallots,** diced

3 cloves **garlic,** minced

6 cups packed **fresh baby spinach**

6 oz (170 g) **shiitake mushrooms** or oyster mushrooms, stemmed and thinly sliced

1 tbsp grated **lemon zest**

1 tsp freshly ground **pepper**

¾ tsp **salt**

4 sides **skinless rainbow trout** (about 10 oz/280 g each)

2 tsp **Dijon mustard**

In saucepan, bring 1½ cups water, wild rice and butter to boil, stirring once; reduce heat, cover and simmer until rice is tender and liquid is absorbed, about 50 minutes.

Meanwhile, heat oil in large skillet over medium heat; cook shallots and garlic, stirring often, until softened and fragrant, about 5 minutes. Add spinach and mushrooms; cook over medium-high heat, stirring often, until spinach is wilted, about 3 minutes. Stir into rice along with lemon zest, half of the pepper and the salt; let cool slightly.

On parchment paper–lined baking sheet, arrange 2 of the sides of trout, fleshy side up and about 2 inches (5 cm) apart. Divide rice mixture evenly over trout to form ½-inch (1 cm) layer, pressing gently to pack down. Arrange remaining trout, fleshy side up, on rice, pressing to adhere.

Spread mustard evenly over trout; sprinkle with remaining pepper.

Bake in 400°F (200°C) oven until trout flakes easily when tested, 20 to 25 minutes. Using large fish spatula or long offset spatula, slide stuffed trout onto large serving platter; cut each stack crosswise into 4 servings.

MAKES 8 SERVINGS. PER SERVING: about 295 cal, 33 g pro, 11 g total fat (3 g sat. fat), 15 g carb, 2 g fibre, 87 mg chol, 310 mg sodium, 881 mg potassium. % RDI: 12% calcium, 12% iron, 35% vit A, 12% vit C, 29% folate.

This delicious stuffing is gluten- and dairy-free (but always check labels of products like broth – or use homemade – to be completely sure). Try it alongside roasted poultry or game birds, or roasted pork. If you use vegetable broth, the stuffing will also be vegetarian.

ROASTED RED PEPPER, FENNEL & BROWN RICE STUFFING

3 **sweet red peppers**

2 small bulbs **fennel**

2 **onions,** chopped

4 cloves **garlic,** sliced

3 tbsp **extra-virgin olive oil**

2 tsp crumbled **dried rosemary**

1¼ tsp **salt**

¾ tsp **pepper**

4 cups **sodium-reduced chicken broth**

1 cup **wild rice**

1¼ cups **brown basmati rice**

½ cup **pine nuts,** toasted

⅓ cup chopped **fresh parsley**

Cut red peppers into 1-inch (2.5 cm) pieces; place in large bowl. Trim tops off fennel bulbs; cut fennel into 1-inch (2.5 cm) chunks and add to bowl. Add onions, garlic, oil, rosemary, ¾ tsp of the salt and pepper; toss well. Spread on large rimmed baking sheet; roast in 425°F (220°C) oven until browned and tender, 40 to 50 minutes.

Meanwhile, in large saucepan, bring broth, wild rice and remaining salt to boil; reduce heat, cover and simmer for 20 minutes.

Stir in brown basmati rice; simmer, covered, until all rice is tender, 15 to 20 minutes. Transfer to bowl.

Add roasted vegetables, pine nuts and parsley; mix well. (Make-ahead: Let cool. Cover and refrigerate for up to 24 hours.)

Spoon stuffing into greased 9-inch (2.5 L) square baking dish. Cover with foil; bake in 400°F (200°C) oven for 20 minutes. Uncover; bake until crisp and golden, about 10 minutes.

MAKES 10 TO 12 SERVINGS. PER EACH OF 12 SERVINGS: about 206 cal, 6 g pro, 8 g total fat (1 g sat. fat), 31 g carb, 4 g fibre, 0 mg chol, 455 mg sodium, 293 mg potassium. % RDI: 3% calcium, 11% iron, 13% vit A, 90% vit C, 14% folate.

Turkey is the go-to holiday meal for many families, and this version is the classic bird your mother or grandmother likely served. It's delicious with Roasted Red Pepper, Fennel & Brown Rice Stuffing (opposite) or Jalapeño Corn Bread Stuffing With Smoked Sausage (page 170).

CLASSIC ROAST TURKEY & GRAVY

15 lb (6.75 kg) **whole turkey**

1 **onion,** quartered

2 ribs **celery,** cut in chunks

2 tsp **dried sage**

1 tsp **dried marjoram**

¼ cup **butter,** melted

½ tsp **pepper**

GRAVY:

2 cups **chicken broth** (approx)

⅓ cup **all-purpose flour**

½ tsp **dried marjoram**

¼ tsp **pepper**

1 tbsp **white wine vinegar**

Remove giblets and neck from turkey; reserve for stock. Pat dry inside and out. Place onion, celery and half each of the sage and marjoram in cavity. Tie legs together; tuck wings under back.

Place turkey, breast side up, on greased rack in roasting pan. Combine butter, pepper and remaining sage and marjoram; brush over turkey.

Roast in 325°F (160°C) oven for 1 hour. Roast, basting often, until meat thermometer inserted in thickest part of thigh registers 185°F (85°C), about 2½ hours. Transfer to cutting board. Tent with foil; let stand for 30 minutes before carving.

GRAVY: Meanwhile, pour pan drippings into large measuring cup; reserving ¼ cup, skim off fat. Add enough of the broth to pan drippings to make 3 cups.

Pour reserved fat back into roasting pan. Stir in flour, marjoram and pepper; cook, stirring, over medium heat for 1 minute.

Gradually whisk in broth mixture and vinegar; bring to boil, stirring and scraping up browned bits. Reduce heat and simmer, stirring often, until thickened, about 10 minutes.

Strain into warmed gravy boat; serve with turkey.

MAKES 16 SERVINGS. PER SERVING: about 561 cal, 69 g pro, 28 g total fat (9 g sat. fat), 2 g carb, trace fibre, 206 mg chol, 277 mg sodium. % RDI: 6% calcium, 33% iron, 1% vit A, 8% folate.

The signature flavour of this fragrant Indian rice dish comes from the combination of a cinnamon stick, a bay leaf and cloves. Although brown basmati rice isn't traditionally used in pilau, it adds fibre and a nice texture. Adding the frozen peas at the end keeps them bright green.

PEAS PILAU

1 **onion**

2 tbsp **butter**

1 clove **garlic,** minced

1 **cinnamon stick,** broken in pieces

4 **green cardamom pods**

4 **whole cloves**

1 **bay leaf**

2 cups **brown basmati rice**

2 cups cold **water**

¾ tsp **salt**

¼ tsp **pepper**

1 cup **frozen peas**

⅓ cup **slivered almonds,** toasted

Cut onion in half. Thinly slice 1 of the halves and set aside. Dice remaining half.

In saucepan, heat 1 tbsp of the butter over medium-high heat; cook diced onion and garlic, stirring occasionally, until softened, about 3 minutes. Add cinnamon, cardamom, cloves and bay leaf; cook until fragrant, about 1 minute.

Stir in rice to coat; toast, stirring, for about 1 minute. Add cold water, ½ tsp of the salt and pepper; bring to boil. Reduce heat, cover and simmer until rice is tender and no liquid remains, 30 to 35 minutes.

Remove from heat. Add peas; fluff with fork. Let stand, covered, for 10 minutes. Discard cinnamon, cardamom, cloves and bay leaf.

Meanwhile, in small skillet, heat remaining butter over medium-high heat; cook sliced onion, stirring occasionally, until golden, about 6 minutes. Stir in almonds and remaining salt. Serve over rice.

MAKES 8 TO 10 SERVINGS. PER EACH OF 10 SERVINGS: about 168 cal, 4 g pro, 5 g total fat (2 g sat. fat), 28 g carb, 3 g fibre, 6 mg chol, 200 mg sodium, 57 mg potassium. % RDI: 1% calcium, 6% iron, 5% vit A, 3% vit C, 5% folate.

This savoury Spanish dish is wonderful for feeding a large group. It gets its signature flavour from saffron, a healthy dose of garlic and zesty chorizo sausage. For this dish, you need the highest-quality semi-dry or dry chorizo you can find: Spanish chorizo or Portuguese chouriço will work equally well. South American–style fresh chorizo, while delicious, doesn't have the right flavour.

BROWN RICE PAELLA

4 cups **sodium-reduced chicken broth**

¼ tsp **saffron threads**

¼ cup **extra-virgin olive oil**

8 oz (225 g) **boneless skinless chicken thighs** (about 4), cut in 1-inch (2.5 cm) chunks

8 oz (225 g) **semi-dry cured chorizo sausage** or dry cured chorizo sausage, thickly sliced

1 **onion,** chopped

1 **sweet yellow pepper,** chopped

6 cloves **garlic,** minced

2 cups **brown basmati rice**

2 tsp **hot smoked paprika**

1 tsp **salt**

½ tsp **pepper**

¾ cup **dry sherry** or dry white wine

8 oz (225 g) **raw large shrimp** (size 31 to 35), peeled and deveined

1¼ cups **frozen peas**

2 cups **cherry tomatoes,** halved

3 tbsp **lemon juice**

¼ cup chopped **fresh parsley**

Stir broth with saffron; set aside.

In deep 12-inch (30 cm) cast-iron skillet or paella pan, heat 1 tbsp of the oil over medium-high heat; brown chicken, about 5 minutes. Transfer to plate. Add 1 tbsp of the remaining oil to pan; brown chorizo, about 5 minutes. Transfer to plate.

Add 1 tbsp of the remaining oil to pan; sauté onion, yellow pepper and garlic until fragrant and beginning to brown, 5 minutes.

Stir in rice, paprika, salt, pepper and remaining oil; cook until rice is coated and toasted, about 5 minutes. Stir in sherry; cook, scraping up browned bits, until almost no liquid remains, about 1 minute.

Return chicken and chorizo to pan along with broth mixture; bring to boil. Reduce heat, cover and simmer until rice is tender and no liquid remains, 50 to 60 minutes.

Stir in shrimp and peas; cover and cook until shrimp is pink and opaque, about 4 minutes.

Stir in tomatoes, lemon juice and parsley.

MAKES 6 TO 8 SERVINGS. PER EACH OF 8 SERVINGS: about 375 cal, 23 g pro, 14 g total fat (2 g sat. fat), 44 g carb, 5 g fibre, 81 mg chol, 1,187 mg sodium, 363 mg potassium. % RDI: 4% calcium, 23% iron, 19% vit A, 67% vit C, 14% folate.

Serve this fragrant East Indian dish with Spinach Raita (opposite), a refreshing palate cleanser. If you like spicy cuisine, increase the number of hot peppers to taste.

SPICED BROWN RICE PILAU WITH EGGPLANT

1 **eggplant** (about 1 lb/450 g)

3 tbsp **vegetable oil**

1 tsp **salt**

3¾ cups warm **water**

2 cups **brown basmati rice**

5 **whole cloves**

5 **green cardamom pods,** cracked

2 **bay leaves**

1 piece (3 inches/8 cm) **cassia bark** or cinnamon stick

1½ tsp **fennel seeds**

½ tsp **cumin seeds**

1 large **onion,** diced

3 cloves **garlic,** minced

1 **green hot pepper,** sliced (and seeded, if desired)

¼ cup minced **fresh cilantro**

2 tbsp **curry paste**

2 tsp minced **fresh ginger**

2 **tomatoes,** each cut in 8 wedges

1 can (19 oz/540 mL) **chickpeas,** drained and rinsed

Fresh cilantro sprigs

Peel and cut eggplant into 1-inch (2.5 cm) cubes; toss with 1 tbsp of the oil and ¼ tsp of the salt. Roast on parchment paper–lined baking sheet in 450°F (230°C) oven until browned, about 20 minutes.

Meanwhile, combine warm water with rice; soak for 10 minutes. Reserving soaking liquid, drain.

In Dutch oven, heat remaining oil over medium heat; fry cloves, cardamom, bay leaves, cassia, fennel seeds and cumin seeds until crackling, about 30 seconds. Add onion; cook, stirring occasionally, until starting to colour, 5 to 6 minutes.

Add garlic, hot pepper, minced cilantro, curry paste, ginger and remaining salt; cook until fragrant, about 2 minutes. Stir in rice until coated; stir in eggplant and tomatoes. Add reserved soaking liquid; bring to boil. Reduce heat, cover and simmer for 30 minutes.

Stir in chickpeas; cook until rice is tender and no liquid remains, about 15 minutes. Fluff with fork. Garnish with cilantro sprigs.

MAKES 6 SERVINGS. PER SERVING: about 440 cal, 10 g pro, 12 g total fat (1 g sat. fat), 73 g carb, 9 g fibre, 0 mg chol, 724 mg sodium. % RDI: 6% calcium, 17% iron, 7% vit A, 23% vit C, 29% folate.

Raita is best made with full-fat Balkan-style yogurt. You can use reduced-fat but not fat-free. Serve this as a cooling, refreshing condiment with Spiced Brown Rice Pilau With Eggplant (opposite) or Whole Grain Vegetable Biryani (page 101).

SPINACH RAITA

1½ cups **plain yogurt**

1 pkg (10 oz/284 g) **fresh spinach,** trimmed

¼ cup chopped **fresh mint** or fresh cilantro

¼ tsp grated **lemon zest**

3 tbsp **lemon juice**

½ tsp **salt**

¼ tsp **pepper**

2 tsp **black mustard seeds** (optional)

In cheesecloth-lined sieve, drain yogurt for 30 minutes.

Rinse spinach; shake off excess water. In large saucepan or Dutch oven over medium-high heat, cook spinach, covered and stirring once, just until wilted, 4 to 5 minutes. Drain and let cool enough to handle; squeeze out liquid. Chop finely.

Mix together spinach, drained yogurt, mint, lemon zest, lemon juice, salt and pepper.

In dry skillet, toast mustard seeds (if using) over medium heat just until grey and crackling, about 3 minutes. Stir into yogurt mixture.

MAKES ABOUT 1¾ CUPS. PER ¼ CUP: about 64 cal, 3 g pro, 3 g total fat (2 g sat. fat), 6 g carb, 1 g fibre, 9 mg chol, 217 mg sodium. % RDI: 12% calcium, 11% iron, 35% vit A, 12% vit C, 28% folate.

For the fresh mushrooms, you can use cremini or button mushrooms, or shiitake caps – whichever kind suits your palate. These pretty crêpes are lovely to serve at a luncheon or as a light dinner.

WILD RICE CRÊPES WITH CHICKEN & MUSHROOMS

1 pkg (14 g) **dried porcini mushrooms**

⅔ cup **boiling water**

1 tbsp **vegetable oil**

3 **boneless skinless chicken breasts,** cut in ¾-inch (2 cm) cubes

2 tbsp **butter**

4 cups thinly sliced **mushrooms**

Half **onion,** diced

½ tsp each **salt** and **pepper**

4 oz (115 g) **light cream cheese**

2 tsp minced **fresh sage** or thyme

½ cup grated **Parmesan cheese**

Wild Rice Crêpes (page 98)

TOMATO RED PEPPER SAUCE:

1 can (14 oz/398 mL) **whole tomatoes**

1 cup drained **jarred roasted red peppers**

Half **onion,** chopped

2 cloves **garlic**

Pinch **hot pepper flakes**

2 tbsp **extra-virgin olive oil**

1 tsp **balsamic vinegar**

¼ tsp **salt**

TOMATO RED PEPPER SAUCE: In blender, purée tomatoes, red peppers, onion, garlic and hot pepper flakes until smooth; pour into saucepan. Add oil, vinegar and salt; bring to boil. Partially cover and simmer until reduced to 2 cups, about 1 hour. *(Make-ahead: Let cool. Refrigerate in airtight container for up to 3 days.)*

Meanwhile, soak dried mushrooms in boiling water until softened, 20 minutes. Reserving soaking liquid, drain. Chop mushrooms.

Meanwhile, in large nonstick skillet, heat oil over medium-high heat; brown chicken. Transfer to bowl.

Add half of the butter to pan; melt over medium-high heat. Sauté porcini and fresh mushrooms, onion, salt and pepper until tender and no liquid remains, 5 minutes.

Cube cream cheese. Return chicken to pan. Stir in cream cheese, sage and reserved soaking liquid; simmer over medium heat until smooth and chicken is no longer pink inside, 3 minutes. Stir in all but 2 tbsp of the Parmesan; let cool slightly.

Spoon about ⅓ cup of the filling down centre of each crêpe; roll up. Arrange crêpes snugly, seam side down and in single layer, in greased 13- x 9-inch (3 L) baking dish. *(Make-ahead: Cover with foil and refrigerate for up to 24 hours; add 10 minutes to baking time, uncovering for last 15 minutes.)*

Melt remaining butter; brush over crêpes. Sprinkle with remaining Parmesan cheese. Bake in 350°F (180°C) oven until hot in centre, 35 minutes. Spoon sauce onto each of 6 plates; top each with 2 crêpes.

MAKES 6 SERVINGS. PER SERVING: about 594 cal, 34 g pro, 31 g total fat (14 g sat. fat), 47 g carb, 4 g fibre, 217 mg chol, 1,112 mg sodium. % RDI: 23% calcium, 30% iron, 36% vit A, 107% vit C, 52% folate.

Nutritious wild rice gives these crêpes an interesting texture. They make a tasty base for savoury Wild Rice Crêpes With Chicken & Mushrooms (page 96), and are also nice rolled around ham and cheese for a simple supper.

WILD RICE CRÊPES

½ cup **wild rice**

¾ tsp **salt**

1⅓ cups **all-purpose flour**

4 **eggs**

1½ cups **milk**

¼ cup **butter,** melted

In saucepan, bring 2 cups water, wild rice and ½ tsp of the salt to boil. Reduce heat, cover and simmer until most of the rice is split and tender, about 45 minutes. Remove from heat; let stand, covered, for 5 minutes. Drain well; let cool.

Meanwhile, in bowl, whisk flour with remaining salt. Whisk together eggs, milk and 2 tbsp of the butter; pour over flour mixture. Whisk until smooth. Strain through fine sieve into bowl. Cover and refrigerate for 1 hour. *(Make-ahead: Refrigerate batter and rice separately for up to 24 hours.)*

Heat 8-inch (20 cm) crêpe pan or skillet over medium heat; brush lightly with some of the remaining butter. Stir rice into batter. For each crêpe, pour ⅓ cup batter into centre of pan; swirl to coat. Cook, turning once, until golden, about 1 minute. Transfer to plate.

Repeat with remaining batter, brushing skillet with some of the remaining butter as needed between batches. *(Make-ahead: Layer between waxed paper and wrap in plastic wrap; refrigerate for up to 3 days or freeze in airtight container for up to 1 month.)*

MAKES 12 CRÊPES. PER CRÊPE: about 148 cal, 5 g pro, 6 g total fat (3 g sat. fat), 17 g carb, 1 g fibre, 75 mg chol, 205 mg sodium. % RDI: 4% calcium, 7% iron, 7% vit A, 20% folate.

Fried rice is an easy way to make leftovers shine. Substitute whatever cooked meat or protein you have on hand for the steak; cubed chicken, pork and tofu are great options. For best results, ensure the rice is cold before stir-frying. Either cook and refrigerate it in the morning or make extra the night before.

STEAK FRIED BROWN RICE

3 tbsp **vegetable oil**

1 **tomato,** diced

3 **green onions**, thinly sliced (white and green parts separated)

3 cloves **garlic,** minced

1 tbsp minced **fresh ginger**

4 **mushrooms,** sliced

1 **carrot,** diced

1 rib **celery,** diced

Half **sweet red pepper,** diced

5 cups cold **cooked brown rice**

2 cups cubed **cooked beef** (steak or roast)

½ cup **frozen peas**

2 tbsp **sodium-reduced soy sauce**

1 tbsp **oyster sauce**

1 tsp **sesame oil**

In wok, heat oil over high heat; stir-fry tomato, white parts of green onions, garlic and ginger for 1 minute.

Add mushrooms, carrot, celery and red pepper; stir-fry until vegetables are tender-crisp, about 4 minutes.

Stir in rice, beef, peas, soy sauce and oyster sauce; stir-fry for 3 minutes. Remove from heat. Stir in green parts of green onions and sesame oil.

MAKES 4 SERVINGS. PER SERVING: about 544 cal, 29 g pro, 18 g total fat (3 g sat. fat), 66 g carb, 6 g fibre, 48 mg chol, 509 mg sodium, 649 mg potassium. % RDI: 6% calcium, 29% iron, 45% vit A, 55% vit C, 20% folate.

This is a risotto you can walk away from without fretting. Brown rice doesn't need a lot of stirring, and it develops just the right amount of chewiness without getting mushy. Asparagus and peas are some of the earliest spring vegetables, so celebrate them with this healthy, hearty dinner.

SPRINGTIME SHRIMP & BROWN RICE RISOTTO

2 tbsp **butter**

1 **onion,** chopped

1 clove **garlic,** minced

2 cups **short-grain brown rice**

1 tsp **salt**

½ tsp **pepper**

¾ cup **dry white wine**

4 cups **sodium-reduced chicken broth**

1 bunch **asparagus** (about 1 lb/ 450 g), trimmed and cut in ½-inch (1 cm) pieces

1½ cups **frozen peas**

½ cup each chopped **fresh mint** and **fresh basil**

½ cup grated **Parmesan cheese**

½ cup **crème fraîche**

2 tsp grated **lemon zest**

1 lb (450 g) **raw large shrimp** (size 31 to 35), peeled and deveined

1 tbsp **olive oil**

Pinch each **salt** and **pepper**

In large skillet, melt butter over medium-high heat; sauté onion and garlic until softened, about 5 minutes.

Stir in brown rice, salt and pepper; cook until rice is coated and slightly toasted, about 3 minutes. Add wine; bring to boil. Boil until reduced by half, about 3 minutes.

Add broth; return to boil. Stir once and reduce heat to medium-low. Cover and simmer until rice is tender, about 50 minutes.

Stir in asparagus and peas; cook until vegetables are tender-crisp, 3 to 5 minutes.

Stir in mint, basil, Parmesan cheese, crème fraîche and lemon zest. Spoon into serving dish; keep warm.

Meanwhile, toss together shrimp, oil, salt and pepper. In skillet, cook shrimp mixture over high heat, turning once, until pink and opaque, about 3 minutes. Serve over risotto.

MAKES 6 SERVINGS. PER SERVING: about 522 cal, 25 g pro, 19 g total fat (10 g sat. fat), 60 g carb, 7 g fibre, 137 mg chol, 1,057 mg sodium, 519 mg potassium. % RDI: 17% calcium, 30% iron, 35% vit A, 17% vit C, 53% folate.

A celebratory dish, biryani is based on the Indian staple basmati rice. Here, brown basmati gives the dish a fibre boost and an earthier flavour that's complemented by the curry spices. This is a hearty, balanced main dish that's perfect for vegetarians.

WHOLE GRAIN VEGETABLE BIRYANI

2 tbsp **extra-virgin olive oil**

1 **onion,** chopped

1 large **carrot,** chopped

2 cloves **garlic,** minced

1 tbsp mild, medium or biryani **curry paste**

¼ tsp each **salt** and **pepper**

1 cup **brown basmati rice**

¾ cup **dried green lentils**

¼ cup **raisins**

2¼ cups **vegetable broth**

2 cups small **cauliflower florets**

1 cup **frozen peas**

¼ cup **sliced almonds** (optional), toasted

In Dutch oven, heat oil over medium-high heat; sauté onion until deep golden, about 6 minutes.

Add carrot, garlic, curry paste, salt and pepper; sauté until fragrant, about 3 minutes. Add rice, lentils and raisins; stir to coat.

Add broth and bring to boil; reduce heat, cover and simmer until rice and vegetables are tender, about 20 minutes.

Stir in cauliflower and peas; cook until heated through and cauliflower is tender-crisp, about 4 minutes. Sprinkle with almonds (if using).

CHANGE IT UP
Whole Grain Chicken Biryani
Omit cauliflower. Cube 2 boneless skinless chicken breasts (12 oz/ 340 g total). Brown in 1 tbsp vegetable oil; remove and set aside. Return to pan along with rice.

TIP: To ensure that the cauliflower florets cook through quickly, cut them no larger than ¾ inch (2 cm).

MAKES 4 SERVINGS. PER SERVING: about 437 cal, 17 g pro, 11 g total fat (1 g sat. fat), 75 g carb, 11 g fibre, 3 mg chol, 731 mg sodium, 672 mg potassium. % RDI: 5% calcium, 38% iron, 49% vit A, 47% vit C, 107% folate.

Nasi goreng is Indonesia's piquant version of fried rice. If you can't find kecap manis in your local Asian grocery store or supermarket, substitute 3 tbsp sodium-reduced soy sauce mixed with 3 tbsp liquid honey.

BROWN RICE NASI GORENG

1 tbsp **olive oil**

3 **eggs,** beaten

1 **onion,** chopped

1 **leek** (white and light green parts only), thinly sliced

Half **sweet red pepper,** thinly sliced

3 cloves **garlic,** minced

1 tsp each **ground cumin** and **ground coriander**

1 tsp **Asian chili paste** (such as sambal oelek)

8 oz (225 g) **boneless skinless chicken thighs,** cubed

8 oz (225 g) **frozen raw large shrimp** (size 31 to 35), thawed, peeled and deveined

3 cups **cooked brown basmati rice**

3 tbsp **kecap manis**

2 tsp **vinegar**

¼ tsp **salt**

3 cups trimmed **fresh spinach leaves,** coarsely chopped

In nonstick wok or deep skillet, heat 1 tsp of the oil over medium heat; cover and cook eggs until firmly set, about 3 minutes. Fold in half and remove from pan; cut into thin strips. Set aside.

In same pan, heat remaining oil over medium-high heat; sauté onion, leek and red pepper until onion begins to soften, about 5 minutes. Stir in garlic, cumin, coriander and chili paste; sauté until fragrant, about 1 minute. Transfer to bowl; set aside.

Add chicken to pan; cook until browned and juices run clear when chicken is pierced, about 5 minutes. Stir in shrimp; cook until pink and opaque, about 1 minute.

Stir in rice, vegetable mixture, kecap manis, vinegar and salt; toss to coat. Stir in spinach; cook until rice is heated through, about 3 minutes. Fold in egg strips.

MAKES 4 SERVINGS. PER SERVING: about 418 cal, 29 g pro, 12 g total fat (3 g sat. fat), 48 g carb, 3 g fibre, 252 mg chol, 788 mg sodium, 550 mg potassium. % RDI: 11% calcium, 33% iron, 37% vit A, 52% vit C, 35% folate.

Kale, brown rice and wild rice team up in this creamy dish that's delicious alongside roast chicken or turkey. Lundberg Wild Blend is a mix of long-grain brown, sweet brown, Wehani, Black Japonica and wild rice. Look for it in natural food stores and large supermarkets.

CREAMY RICE & KALE CASSEROLE

1 bunch **kale,** trimmed and stems removed

3 cups **sodium-reduced chicken broth**

1½ cups **brown and wild rice blend** (such as Lundberg Wild Blend)

1 tbsp **butter**

1 **onion,** chopped

3 cloves **garlic,** finely chopped

3 tbsp **all-purpose flour**

2 cups **milk**

1 tsp chopped **fresh thyme**

½ tsp each **salt** and **pepper**

¾ cup **light cream cheese,** softened

1 cup grated **Parmesan cheese**

* TIP: Cream cheese usually comes in 250 g blocks that have cup measurements marked on the side. Three-quarters of a 250 g package equals ¾ cup.

In large pot of boiling water, blanch kale until wilted and tender, about 1 minute. Drain and squeeze out excess moisture; roughly chop. Set aside.

In large saucepan, bring broth and rice blend to boil, stirring once. Reduce heat, cover and simmer until rice is tender and no liquid remains, about 50 minutes.

Meanwhile, in separate saucepan, melt butter over medium-high heat; sauté onion and garlic until softened, about 8 minutes.

Add flour; cook, stirring, until incorporated, 2 minutes. Slowly whisk in milk, thyme, salt and pepper. Bring to boil; reduce heat and simmer until thick enough to coat back of spoon, 10 minutes.

To rice, add sauce, kale, cream cheese and half of the Parmesan cheese; stir until well combined and cheese is melted. Scrape into 8-inch (2 L) square baking dish; sprinkle remaining Parmesan cheese over top.

Bake in top third of 375°F (190°C) oven until sauce is bubbly, about 20 minutes. Broil until top is golden, about 3 minutes.

MAKES 8 TO 10 SERVINGS. PER EACH OF 10 SERVINGS: about 242 cal, 12 g pro, 10 g total fat (5 g sat. fat), 31 g carb, 3 g fibre, 29 mg chol, 576 mg sodium, 278 mg potassium. % RDI: 21% calcium, 7% iron, 47% vit A, 48% vit C, 7% folate.

A simple flavoured pilaf – with the delicious addition of chewy whole grain wild rice – makes a great side dish to serve with Classic Roast Turkey & Gravy (page 89). Use fresh walnut halves from California for the nicest flavour.

BASMATI & WILD RICE PILAF WITH SPINACH & WALNUTS

⅔ cup **wild rice**

3 tbsp **vegetable oil**

1 **onion,** finely diced

1 **green onion,** thinly sliced (white and green parts separated)

1 **bay leaf**

½ tsp **salt**

¼ tsp **pepper**

3 cups **basmati rice**

2 cups trimmed **fresh spinach leaves,** finely chopped

1 cup **walnuts,** toasted and coarsely chopped

¼ cup chopped **fresh parsley**

In saucepan of boiling salted water, cook wild rice until tender, about 40 minutes. Drain; set aside.

In separate saucepan, heat oil over medium-high heat; sauté onion, white part of green onion, bay leaf, salt and pepper until softened and just beginning to turn golden, about 5 minutes.

Stir in basmati rice; cook, stirring, for 1 minute.

Stir in 3½ cups water; bring to boil. Reduce heat, cover and simmer until no liquid remains and rice is tender, 12 to 14 minutes. Turn off heat.

Stir in spinach, walnuts, parsley, green part of green onion and wild rice; cover and let stand on turned-off burner for 5 minutes. Discard bay leaf.

MAKES 12 SERVINGS. PER SERVING: about 300 cal, 7 g pro, 10 g total fat (1 g sat. fat), 46 g carb, 2 g fibre, 0 mg chol, 223 mg sodium, 167 mg potassium. % RDI: 3% calcium, 7% iron, 6% vit A, 3% vit C, 15% folate.

Pepitas, or unsalted raw hulled green pumpkin seeds, add a nice crunch to nutty-tasting wild rice. Try this side dish with grilled or roasted meats or poultry. It's an instant classic.

WILD RICE WITH PEPITAS

¼ cup **pepitas** (unsalted raw hulled pumpkin seeds) or chopped pecans

1 cup **wild rice**

1 tbsp **butter**

1 small **onion,** chopped

1 each small **carrot** and rib **celery,** finely diced

Half **sweet yellow pepper,** diced

½ tsp each **salt** and **pepper**

In dry small skillet, toast pepitas over medium heat until fragrant, about 8 minutes. *(Make-ahead: Set aside for up to 24 hours.)*

In large saucepan of boiling salted water, cover and cook wild rice just until tender and beginning to split, about 1 hour. Drain in sieve and set aside.

In same saucepan, melt butter over medium heat; fry onion, carrot, celery, yellow pepper, salt and pepper, stirring often, until softened, about 7 minutes.

Stir in rice. *(Make-ahead: Let cool. Cover and refrigerate for up to 24 hours. Add 2 tbsp water.)* Cook until heated through; stir in pepitas.

MAKES 4 SERVINGS. PER SERVING: about 240 cal, 7 g pro, 9 g total fat (2 g sat. fat), 36 g carb, 4 g fibre, 9 mg chol, 342 mg sodium. % RDI: 2% calcium, 10% iron, 49% vit A, 40% vit C, 22% folate.

Since cooked rice hardens in the refrigerator, this dish tastes best when the rice is freshly made. This salad is a tasty alternative to plain rice or potatoes as a side dish.

BROWN BASMATI & WILD RICE SALAD

1¼ cups **brown basmati rice**

1 cup **wild rice**

½ tsp **salt**

2 **carrots,** halved lengthwise and sliced

1 cup **slivered almonds,** toasted

¾ cup thinly sliced **radishes** (about 6)

6 **green onions,** thinly sliced

DRESSING:
1 clove **garlic,** minced

⅓ cup **white balsamic vinegar**

¼ cup **extra-virgin olive oil**

1 tbsp **Dijon mustard**

¼ tsp each **salt** and **pepper**

In large saucepan, bring 4 cups water, basmati rice, wild rice and salt to boil; reduce heat, cover and simmer until all rice is tender, 40 to 50 minutes. Transfer to bowl.

DRESSING: Meanwhile, whisk together garlic, vinegar, oil, mustard, salt and pepper; pour over rice and toss to coat. Let stand for 30 minutes.

Add carrots, almonds, radishes and green onions; toss to combine. *(Make-ahead: Cover and let stand for up to 1 hour.)*

MAKES 10 TO 12 SERVINGS. PER EACH OF 12 SERVINGS: about 214 cal, 6 g pro, 10 g total fat (1 g sat. fat), 28 g carb, 3 g fibre, 0 mg chol, 177 mg sodium, 188 mg potassium. % RDI: 3% calcium, 9% iron, 22% vit A, 5% vit C, 10% folate.

Asian accents give this rice salad a unique twist. If you have leftover smoked turkey or chicken, this is a delicious way to use it up.

SMOKED TURKEY RICE SALAD

¼ tsp **salt**

1 cup **parboiled brown rice**

¼ cup **sesame seeds**

2 cups cubed **smoked turkey thigh** or ham

2 cups **bean sprouts**

1 **sweet yellow pepper,** diced

2 **green onions,** sliced

⅓ cup **raisins** (optional)

8 leaves **Boston lettuce**

DRESSING:

⅓ cup **orange juice**

1 tbsp each **soy sauce** and **sesame oil**

1 tsp grated **fresh ginger**

1 clove **garlic,** minced

Pinch each **salt** and **pepper**

In saucepan, bring 2 cups water and salt to boil; add rice. Cover and reduce heat to medium-low; cook until tender and water is absorbed, about 20 minutes. Remove from heat; let stand for 5 minutes.

Meanwhile, in dry skillet, toast sesame seeds over low heat until golden; set aside.

DRESSING: In large bowl, whisk together orange juice, soy sauce, sesame oil, ginger, garlic, salt and pepper.

To dressing, add rice, turkey, bean sprouts, yellow pepper, green onions, raisins (if using) and sesame seeds; toss to combine. Serve on lettuce.

MAKES 4 SERVINGS. PER SERVING: about 414 cal, 26 g pro, 15 g total fat (3 g sat. fat), 45 g carb, 4 g fibre, 73 mg chol, 476 mg sodium. % RDI: 7% calcium, 28% iron, 3% vit A, 120% vit C, 40% folate.

Curry spices are a natural match for lentils. Here, the pair is further complemented by a mix of chewy wild rice and tender orzo pasta. The salad is a nice partner to grilled or roasted meats, but a larger portion also makes a satisfying vegetarian main dish.

CURRIED LENTIL, WILD RICE & ORZO SALAD

½ cup **wild rice**

⅔ cup **dried green lentils** or dried brown lentils

½ cup **orzo pasta**

½ cup **dried currants**

¼ cup finely chopped **red onion**

⅓ cup **slivered almonds,** toasted

DRESSING:

¼ cup **white wine vinegar**

1 tsp **ground cumin**

1 tsp **Dijon mustard**

½ tsp **granulated sugar**

½ tsp **salt**

½ tsp **ground coriander**

¼ tsp **turmeric**

¼ tsp **sweet paprika**

¼ tsp **nutmeg**

Pinch each **cinnamon, ground cloves** and **cayenne pepper**

⅓ cup **canola oil** or vegetable oil

In large pot of boiling salted water, cover and cook wild rice for 10 minutes.

Add lentils; boil for 20 minutes. Add orzo; cook just until tender, about 5 minutes. Drain well and transfer to large bowl. Add currants and onion.

DRESSING: In small bowl, whisk together vinegar, cumin, mustard, sugar, salt, coriander, turmeric, paprika, nutmeg, cinnamon, cloves and cayenne pepper; whisk in oil. Pour over warm rice mixture and toss gently to coat.

Let cool; cover and refrigerate until chilled, about 4 hours. *(Make-ahead: Refrigerate for up to 24 hours.)*

To serve, sprinkle with almonds.

MAKES 12 SERVINGS. PER SERVING: about 178 cal, 6 g pro, 8 g total fat (1 g sat. fat), 22 g carb, 3 g fibre, 0 mg chol, 178 mg sodium, 231 mg potassium. % RDI: 2% calcium, 13% iron, 2% vit C, 30% folate.

PROFILE:
WILD RICE

WHY IT'S GOOD FOR YOU: Sure, it's more expensive than brown or white rice but, for its nutritional value, wild rice is worth every extra nickel. Native to Canada, wild rice thrives in Manitoba's ancient mineral bedrock. It beats white rice hands down for protein, vitamin E, magnesium, phosphorus, zinc and folic acid. It's also a delicious gluten-free option for people with celiac disease or gluten sensitivity.

WHOLE GRAIN FORMS: Glossy, dark **wild rice** is called a grain but is actually the whole, unrefined seeds of the wild rice plant, an aquatic grass. **Wild rice blends** are widely available in grocery stores. These mix wild rice with brown rice and exotic red and/or black rice varieties for added flavour. **Pasta** made from wild rice is sometimes available in health food stores and supermarkets. It's a gluten-free alternative to wheat pasta. **Whole grain flour** made from ground wild rice can be used in gluten-free baking. Like other gluten-free flours, it needs to be paired with other flours or ingredients to make breads, cakes and other treats rise.

STORAGE: Wild rice is more shelf-stable than other whole grains. Seal it in an airtight container and keep it in a cool, dark, dry place for up to a year.

USES: Wild rice has a rich, nutty flavour and a pleasant chewy texture. It's ideal in pilafs, salads and stuffings, and is a delicious addition to soups. Use wild rice pasta and flour in gluten-free main dishes and baked goods, respectively.

Clockwise from top left:
Wild rice, wild rice blend,
whole grain wild rice flour
and wild rice fusilli pasta

Toasting corn and beans brings out their flavours and transforms this dish into an exotic South American–style salad.

BROWN RICE & TOASTED BEAN SALAD

1 cup **brown rice**

1 cup **frozen corn kernels,** thawed

3 large **plum tomatoes,** halved lengthwise

6 **green onions**

1 can (19 oz/540 mL) **black beans,** drained and rinsed

¾ tsp each **dried oregano** and **ground cumin**

3 cups **baby arugula**

⅔ cup **unsalted roasted hulled pumpkin seeds** or sliced almonds

⅔ cup crumbled **feta cheese**

½ cup chopped **fresh cilantro**

DRESSING:

⅓ cup **extra-virgin olive oil**

3 tbsp **lime juice**

1 clove **garlic,** minced

½ tsp each **salt** and **pepper**

DRESSING: Whisk together olive oil, lime juice, garlic, salt and pepper; set aside.

In saucepan, bring rice and 2 cups water to boil; reduce heat, cover and simmer until no liquid remains, 30 to 35 minutes. Let cool for 10 minutes; fluff with fork.

Meanwhile, in dry cast-iron or other heavy skillet, toast corn over high heat, shaking pan, until fragrant and lightly charred, 1 to 2 minutes. Transfer to large bowl.

In same skillet, cook tomatoes and green onions, turning once, until softened and lightly charred, about 3 minutes. Let cool on cutting board; cut into small chunks and add to bowl.

Add black beans, oregano and cumin to skillet; cook until beans are dry and fragrant, about 2 minutes. Add to bowl. Stir in rice, arugula and pumpkin seeds.

Add dressing, feta cheese and cilantro; toss to coat.

MAKES 4 SERVINGS. PER SERVING: about 758 cal, 30 g pro, 42 g total fat (10 g sat. fat), 74 g carb, 18 g fibre, 23 mg chol, 959 mg sodium, 1,154 mg potassium. % RDI: 26% calcium, 73% iron, 23% vit A, 37% vit C, 75% folate.

Wild rice naturally complements the woodsy flavour of mushrooms. A small amount of cream enriches the soup at the end of cooking but doesn't make it heavy. Serve with slices of Wild Rice Walnut Bâtard (page 115).

WILD RICE MUSHROOM SOUP

2 cups cold **water**

½ cup **wild rice**

1¼ tsp **salt**

1 pkg (14 g) **dried porcini mushrooms**

1 cup **boiling water**

1 tbsp **vegetable oil**

2 tbsp **butter**

4 cups sliced **cremini mushrooms**

¼ cup **brandy**

2 cups finely chopped **onions**

2 cups finely chopped **celery**

2 cloves **garlic,** minced

1 tbsp chopped **fresh thyme** (or 1 tsp dried thyme)

¼ tsp **pepper**

2 cups **sodium-reduced chicken broth** or vegetable broth

¼ cup **whipping cream** (35%)

In saucepan, bring cold water, wild rice and ½ tsp of the salt to boil. Reduce heat, cover and simmer until most of the rice is split and tender, 45 minutes. Remove from heat; let stand, covered, for 5 minutes. Drain. *(Make-ahead: Let cool for 30 minutes; refrigerate in airtight container for up to 2 days.)*

Meanwhile, in heatproof bowl, soak dried mushrooms in boiling water until softened, about 30 minutes. Reserving soaking liquid, strain, discarding sediment.

In skillet, heat oil and half of the butter over medium-high heat; sauté cremini mushrooms, porcini mushrooms and ¼ tsp of the remaining salt until golden, about 5 minutes. Add brandy; cook until most of the liquid is evaporated, about 1 minute. Set aside.

In large saucepan, melt remaining butter over medium heat; fry onions, celery, garlic, thyme, pepper and remaining salt, stirring often, until vegetables are very soft, about 10 minutes.

Add reserved soaking liquid, broth and 2 cups water; bring to boil. Reduce heat and simmer, uncovered and stirring occasionally, for 20 minutes. Stir in mushrooms; let cool slightly.

In blender, purée half of the soup; return to saucepan. Stir in wild rice and cream; bring to simmer over medium heat, stirring often. *(Make-ahead: Let cool for 30 minutes; refrigerate, uncovered, in airtight container until cold. Cover and refrigerate for up to 2 days.)*

MAKES 6 SERVINGS. PER SERVING: about 199 cal, 5 g pro, 10 g total fat (5 g sat. fat), 21 g carb, 4 g fibre, 25 mg chol, 767 mg sodium. % RDI: 5% calcium, 6% iron, 7% vit A, 12% vit C, 18% folate.

This robust soup is so flavourful because it uses homemade turkey stock, which is a snap to make in a slow cooker after a roast turkey dinner. For this recipe, you need almost a double batch, so make and freeze extra ahead of time. If you want to use leftover cooked turkey, skip the browning step and add it straight to the soup.

TURKEY & WILD RICE SOUP

1½ lb (675 g) **boneless skinless turkey breast** or turkey thigh, cut in small chunks

1 tsp each **salt** and **pepper**

1½ tbsp **olive oil**

1 large **carrot,** diced

1 **parsnip,** diced

1 rib **celery,** diced

1 **onion,** diced

1 clove **garlic,** minced

8 cups **Slow-Cooker Turkey Stock** (right)

1 cup **brown and wild rice blend** (such as Lundberg Wild Blend)

1 tsp **fresh thyme**

2 cups **green cabbage,** chopped

2 tbsp chopped **fresh parsley**

1 tbsp **lemon juice**

Sprinkle turkey with pinch each of the salt and pepper. In large Dutch oven, heat oil over medium-high heat; brown turkey, in 2 batches, about 5 minutes. Transfer to plate.

Add carrot, parsnip, celery, onion and garlic to pan; cook, stirring occasionally, until softened, about 5 minutes.

Stir in remaining salt and pepper; return turkey and any accumulated juices to pan. Add stock, rice blend and thyme; bring to boil. Reduce heat and simmer until rice is tender and soup is slightly thickened, about 50 minutes.

Add cabbage; cook, stirring, until wilted, about 3 minutes. Stir in parsley and lemon juice.

MAKE YOUR OWN
Slow-Cooker Turkey Stock
In slow cooker, combine 1 turkey carcass, broken in 3 or 4 pieces; 2 ribs celery with leaves, coarsely chopped; 2 each carrots and onions (unpeeled), coarsely chopped; 1 bay leaf; 1 tbsp black peppercorns; and 6 stems fresh parsley or cilantro. Pour in 8 cups water. Cover; cook on low for 8 to 10 hours. Strain through cheesecloth-lined sieve set over large bowl; let cool. Refrigerate until fat solidifies on surface, about 8 hours. Discard fat. *(Make-ahead: Refrigerate in airtight container for up to 3 days or freeze for up to 4 months.)*

MAKES 6 CUPS.

MAKES 8 SERVINGS. PER SERVING: about 238 cal, 23 g pro, 5 g total fat (1 g sat. fat), 26 g carb, 3 g fibre, 44 mg chol, 423 mg sodium, 532 mg potassium. % RDI: 3% calcium, 10% iron, 21% vit A, 13% vit C, 12% folate.

Wild rice adds chewy texture and rich flavour to this rustic, wholesome bread. The bâtard shape (oval with pointed ends) lends the loaf an artisanal French bakery touch.

WILD RICE WALNUT BÂTARD

1 tsp **granulated sugar**

2¼ cups warm **water**

1 pkg (8 g) **active dry yeast** (2¼ tsp)

3 tbsp **liquid honey**

2 tbsp **vegetable oil**

2 tsp **salt**

3 cups **multigrain bread flour** (such as Robin Hood Best for Bread Multigrain Blend)

2¼ cups **white bread flour** (approx)

1½ cups **cooked wild rice**

¾ cup coarsely chopped **walnuts,** toasted

✳ TIP: To cook the amount of wild rice you need for this recipe, in saucepan, bring 2 cups cold water, ½ cup wild rice and ½ tsp salt to boil. Reduce heat, cover and simmer until most of the rice is split and tender, 45 minutes. Remove from heat; let stand, covered, for 5 minutes. Drain. *(Make-ahead: Let cool for 30 minutes; refrigerate in airtight container for up to 2 days.)*

In large bowl, dissolve sugar in ½ cup of the warm water. Sprinkle in yeast; let stand until frothy, about 10 minutes. Stir in remaining water, honey, oil and salt. Stir in multigrain flour and 1½ cups of the white bread flour, 1 cup at a time, to make slightly sticky dough. Stir in rice and nuts.

Turn out onto floured surface; knead, adding remaining white flour as needed to prevent sticking, until smooth and elastic, 10 minutes. Place in greased bowl; turn to grease all over. Cover and let rise in warm place until doubled in bulk, 1¼ hours.

Punch down dough; turn out onto floured surface. Divide into thirds. Pat each into 9- x 5-inch (23 x 12 cm) rectangle; starting at long side, tightly roll up.

Shape each into thick elongated torpedo shape; pinch seams. Place on parchment paper–lined baking sheets; cover and let rise in warm place until doubled in bulk, about 45 minutes. Generously dust with some of the remaining white flour; with serrated knife, cut 3 crosswise slashes in top of each.

Place racks in top and bottom thirds of oven; heat to 400°F (200°C). Spritz oven with cold water (avoiding lightbulb) 6 to 10 times until steamy. Immediately place bread in oven; repeat steaming after 3 minutes. Bake, rotating and switching pans halfway through, until loaves sound hollow when tapped on bottoms, 40 minutes. Let cool on racks. *(Make-ahead: Store in airtight container for up to 2 days. Or wrap in plastic wrap then heavy-duty foil; freeze for up to 2 weeks.)*

MAKES 3 LOAVES, 12 SLICES EACH. PER SLICE: about 108 cal, 3 g pro, 3 g total fat (trace sat. fat), 18 g carb, 1 g fibre, 0 mg chol, 161 mg sodium. % RDI: 1% calcium, 7% iron, 9% folate.

Tuck one of these delightful homemade snacks into your lunch bag or your kid's backpack for a nutritious afternoon pick-me-up. When the honey boils down, it gets thick, syrupy and surprisingly less sticky. You can add nuts to these if you like; just substitute ½ cup of them for the pumpkin seeds.

MULTISEED CRANBERRY ENERGY BARS

½ cup **unsalted roasted hulled sunflower seeds**

½ cup **unsalted roasted hulled pumpkin seeds**

¼ cup **sesame seeds**

4 cups **puffed brown rice**

1 cup **dried cranberries**

1 cup **liquid honey**

½ tsp **sea salt** or kosher salt

Spread sunflower seeds, pumpkin seeds and sesame seeds on rimmed baking sheet. Bake in 350°F (180°C) oven until lightly toasted, about 6 minutes. Let cool. Transfer to large well-greased bowl. Add puffed brown rice and cranberries to bowl.

In large saucepan, boil honey with salt over medium heat, without stirring, for 5 minutes. Stir into puffed rice mixture until rice is well coated.

Immediately scrape into greased 13- x 9-inch (3.5 L) cake pan, pressing to smooth and level top. Let cool.

With greased knife, cut into bars. *(Make-ahead: Store individually wrapped bars in airtight container for up to 2 weeks.)*

MAKES 24 BARS. PER BAR: about 101 cal, 2 g pro, 3 g total fat (trace sat. fat), 19 g carb, 1 g fibre, 0 mg chol, 49 mg sodium, 62 mg potassium. % RDI: 1% calcium, 6% iron, 4% folate.

Wild rice is native to Canada, and it's an important part of the nation's food history. Using a blend of brown and wild rice, such as Lundberg Wild Blend, gives this classic comfort-food dessert a healthy boost of fibre and a slight chewiness. If you love ginger, top the pudding with extra crystallized ginger.

COCONUT GINGER WILD RICE PUDDING

1 cup **brown and wild rice blend** (such as Lundberg Wild Blend)

2 cups **milk**

1 can (400 mL) **light coconut milk**

⅓ cup **granulated sugar**

3 tbsp chopped **crystallized ginger**

¼ tsp **cinnamon**

¼ tsp **ground cardamom**

Pinch **salt**

¼ cup **unsweetened desiccated coconut,** toasted

¼ cup chopped **pistachios,** toasted

In food processor, pulse rice until grains just begin to break up, about 30 seconds.

In saucepan, bring milk and rice to boil, stirring once; reduce heat, cover and simmer until rice is tender and liquid is absorbed, 30 to 40 minutes.

Stir in coconut milk, sugar, ginger, cinnamon, cardamom and salt; reduce heat, cover and simmer over very low heat until thick enough to mound on spoon, 20 to 30 minutes.

Spoon into dessert bowls; sprinkle with coconut and pistachios.

TIP: To toast the pistachios and coconut, arrange separately on rimmed baking sheet; toast in 350°F (180°C) oven until coconut is golden, about 5 minutes.

MAKES 6 TO 8 SERVINGS. PER EACH OF 8 SERVINGS: about 233 cal, 5 g pro, 9 g total fat (5 g sat. fat), 36 g carb, 2 g fibre, 5 mg chol, 39 mg sodium, 278 mg potassium. % RDI: 8% calcium, 11% iron, 3% vit A, 3% vit C, 2% folate.

BUCKWHEAT & RYE

Buckwheat flour has a strong flavour, but mixing it with all-purpose flour makes it a little gentler. Buckwheat honey also has a deep, dark flavour that's really wonderful, but feel free to substitute another favourite type of honey if you prefer.

BUCKWHEAT HONEY PANCAKES

1 **egg**

1½ cups **milk**

2 tbsp **butter,** melted, or vegetable oil

1 tbsp **buckwheat honey** or other liquid honey

¾ cup **dark buckwheat flour**

¾ cup **all-purpose flour**

1 tbsp **baking powder**

½ tsp **salt**

In large bowl, beat together egg, milk, butter and honey. Whisk together buckwheat and all-purpose flours, baking powder and salt; pour over egg mixture and stir until almost smooth.

Lightly brush large nonstick skillet with oil or butter; heat over medium heat. Using ¼ cup for each pancake, pour in batter, spreading with spatula to 4-inch (10 cm) diameter. Cook until underside is golden and bubbles break on top that do not fill in, 1½ to 2 minutes.

Turn pancakes; cook until underside is golden, 30 to 60 seconds.

Repeat with remaining batter, brushing skillet with more oil or butter as needed between batches.

MAKES 12 PANCAKES. PER PANCAKE: about 99 cal, 3 g pro, 3 g total fat (2 g sat. fat), 15 g carb, 1 g fibre, 23 mg chol, 203 mg sodium, 107 mg potassium. % RDI: 7% calcium, 6% iron, 4% vit A, 10% folate.

This crunchy granola is great with yogurt. Look for buckwheat flakes in the cereal aisles of health food stores; kasha, or roasted buckwheat groats, are available in supermarkets. Seeds are high in fat, so this recipe doesn't call for extra oil – but you'd never know it from the taste.

GLUTEN-FREE BUCKWHEAT GRANOLA

2 cups **wheat-free rolled oats**

1 cup **kasha**

1 cup **rolled buckwheat flakes**

1 cup **unsalted roasted hulled pumpkin seeds**

½ cup **unsalted roasted hulled sunflower seeds**

¼ cup **amaranth**

½ cup **liquid honey**

½ cup **brown rice syrup**

1 cup chopped **dried apples**

1 cup **dried cranberries**

In large bowl, mix together oats, kasha, buckwheat flakes, pumpkin seeds, sunflower seeds and amaranth. Stir in honey and brown rice syrup until coated; spread evenly on parchment paper–lined rimmed baking sheets.

Bake in 275°F (140°C) oven, stirring occasionally, until golden, about 1 hour.

Let cool completely on pans on racks. Stir in apples and cranberries. (*Make-ahead: Store in airtight container for up 1 month.*)

MAKES ABOUT 6 CUPS. PER ¼ CUP: about 204 cal, 7 g pro, 6 g total fat (1 g sat. fat), 34 g carb, 4 g fibre, 0 mg chol, 13 mg sodium, 169 mg potassium. % RDI: 2% calcium, 18% iron, 8% folate.

You might as well make a big batch of granola while you're at it. This recipe makes 5 cups – plenty for this breakfast and many more. Individually quick frozen (IQF) berry mixes are excellent when berries aren't in season; they will give you the best firm, whole-berry texture.

BERRY BREAKFAST SUNDAES

3 cups **Balkan-style plain yogurt**

1 tsp finely grated **lemon zest**

1 tsp **lemon juice**

TWO-BERRY GRANOLA:

¼ cup **vegetable oil**

1 cup **large-flake rolled oats**

1 cup **rolled rye flakes**

⅓ cup **unsweetened desiccated coconut**

⅓ cup **unsalted roasted hulled sunflower seeds**

⅓ cup **slivered almonds** (optional)

¾ cup **liquid honey**

½ cup each **dried blueberries** and **dried cranberries**

MIXED BERRY SAUCE:

3 cups fresh or thawed **mixed berries** (raspberries, blueberries, blackberries and quartered strawberries)

2 tbsp **granulated sugar**

2 tbsp **black currant juice** (such as Ribena) or lemon juice

TWO-BERRY GRANOLA: Line rimmed baking sheet with heavy-duty or double-thickness foil; brush with 1 tbsp of the oil. Set aside. In large bowl, toss together oats, rye flakes, coconut, sunflower seeds, and almonds (if using). Whisk together honey, remaining oil and 1 cup water; pour over oat mixture and toss to combine. Spread on prepared pan.

Bake in 275°F (140°C) oven, stirring every 15 minutes, until liquid is evaporated and granola clumps together, about 2 hours. Let cool on pan on rack. Break apart large clumps; stir in blueberries and cranberries. Set aside 1 cup; store remainder for another use in airtight container for up to 2 weeks.

Meanwhile, line sieve with double-thickness cheesecloth; set over bowl. Spoon in yogurt; cover and drain in refrigerator until reduced to about 2 cups, 1 hour. *(Make-ahead: Cover and refrigerate for up to 24 hours.)*

Stir together drained yogurt, lemon zest and lemon juice.

MIXED BERRY SAUCE: Meanwhile, place 2¾ cups of the berries in large bowl. In separate bowl, crush remaining berries with fork; stir in sugar and black currant juice until dissolved. Add to whole berries and toss. *(Make-ahead: Cover and refrigerate for up to 24 hours.)*

In each of 4 parfait glasses, layer about ¼ cup yogurt mixture, ¼ cup berry sauce and 2 tbsp of the reserved granola; repeat layers once.

MAKES 4 SERVINGS. PER SERVING: about 412 cal, 11 g pro, 17 g total fat (8 g sat. fat), 55 g carb, 7 g fibre, 31 mg chol, 74 mg sodium. % RDI: 27% calcium, 10% iron, 9% vit A, 63% vit C, 20% folate.

Buckwheat and whole wheat flours make these waffles hearty, but they still come out light and fluffy. To make plain waffles, just omit the berries. The plain version makes a nice base for eggs Benedict, or it can stand in for bread to make unique breakfast sandwiches.

BERRY BUCKWHEAT WAFFLES

1 cup **dark buckwheat flour**

1 cup **whole wheat flour**

1 tbsp **baking powder**

2 tsp **granulated sugar**

1 tsp **baking soda**

½ tsp **salt**

2 **eggs,** separated

2¼ cups **buttermilk**

¼ cup **butter,** melted

½ cup chopped **fresh strawberries**

½ cup **fresh blueberries**

In large bowl, whisk together buckwheat and whole wheat flours, baking powder, sugar, baking soda and salt. In separate bowl, whisk together egg yolks, buttermilk, ¼ cup water and butter. Set aside.

Beat egg whites until stiff peaks form. Stir milk mixture into dry ingredients just until smooth. Stir in strawberries and blueberries. Fold in egg whites.

Heat waffle iron according to manufacturer's instructions; grease. Using about ½ cup per waffle (see Tip, left), pour batter onto waffle iron, spreading to edges. Close lid and cook until crisp, golden and steam stops, about 5 minutes.

TIP: The amount of batter you'll use per waffle depends on the size of your waffle iron. Aim to cover about three-quarters of the iron with batter before closing the lid. If batter leaks out the side, reduce the amount for the next waffle.

MAKES 8 TO 10 WAFFLES. PER EACH OF 10 WAFFLES: about 178 cal, 7 g pro, 7 g total fat (4 g sat. fat), 23 g carb, 3 g fibre, 54 mg chol, 395 mg sodium, 251 mg potassium. % RDI: 11% calcium, 9% iron, 6% vit A, 7% vit C, 8% folate.

Tiny buckwheat pancakes are the ideal backdrop for a curl of tender, salty-sweet cured salmon. If you just can't wait five days, you can eat the gravlax as early as the third day of curing.

GRAVLAX BLINI BITES

1 tbsp **black peppercorns**

⅓ cup **granulated sugar**

¼ cup **pickling salt** or kosher salt

2 lb (900 g) **skin-on centre-cut salmon fillet**

⅓ cup chopped **fresh dill**

2 tbsp **brandy** or aquavit

Small **fresh dill sprigs**

MUSTARD SAUCE:

3 tbsp **Dijon mustard**

2 tbsp **liquid honey**

1 tbsp chopped **fresh dill**

BUCKWHEAT BLINIS:

1½ tsp **granulated sugar**

¼ cup warm **water**

1½ tsp **active dry yeast**

1 **egg**

1½ cups lukewarm **milk**

1 cup **all-purpose flour**

¾ cup **dark buckwheat flour**

½ tsp **salt**

¼ cup **butter,** melted

Coarsely crush peppercorns. Mix peppercorns, sugar and salt; spread over both sides of salmon. Spread one-third of the chopped dill down centre of large piece of plastic wrap; top with fish, skin side down.

Drizzle with brandy; spread remaining chopped dill over top. Wrap tightly in plastic wrap; place on small rimmed baking sheet. Place small cutting board on fish; weigh down with 2 full 28-oz (796 mL) cans. Refrigerate for 5 days, turning fish daily.

MUSTARD SAUCE: Stir together mustard, honey and dill. *(Make-ahead: Cover and refrigerate for up to 3 days.)*

BUCKWHEAT BLINIS: In small bowl, dissolve ½ tsp of the sugar in warm water. Sprinkle in yeast; let stand until frothy, about 10 minutes.

In separate bowl, beat egg, milk and remaining sugar. Add all-purpose flour, buckwheat flour and salt; beat for 1 minute. Beat in yeast mixture and half of the butter. Cover; let rise in warm place until doubled, 1 hour.

Brush nonstick skillet with some of the remaining butter; heat over medium heat. Without stirring, spoon batter into pan by scant 2 tbsp. Cook until bubbles break on top that do not fill in, 1 minute. Flip; cook until bottom is golden, about 30 seconds. Repeat with remaining butter and batter.

Unwrap fish; brush off most of the dill. *(Make-ahead: Wrap in plastic wrap and refrigerate for up to 5 days.)* Slice thinly on 45-degree angle; cut each slice in half and place on blini. Drizzle with mustard sauce; garnish each with dill sprig.

MAKES ABOUT 50 PIECES. PER PIECE: about 71 cal, 5 g pro, 3 g total fat (1 g sat. fat), 6 g carb, trace fibre, 18 mg chol, 594 mg sodium. % RDI: 1% calcium, 2% iron, 2% vit A, 2% vit C, 5% folate.

If you're looking for a light-tasting dinner that's packed with nutrients, this is your dish. Soba noodles are made from buckwheat flour and don't require much time for cooking. Japanese or other Asian grocery stores carry many of these ingredients, but more and more supermarkets are beginning to stock them, too.

SOBA NOODLES WITH SPINACH & TOFU

1 pkg (8 oz/250 g) **soba noodles**

1 lb (450 g) **fresh spinach,** trimmed

1 pkg (10 oz/300 g) **soft tofu,** cubed

2 **green onions,** thinly sliced diagonally

2 tbsp **thin nori strips** (optional)

1 tbsp toasted **sesame seeds**

SOBA SAUCE:

1 piece (about 4 inches/10 cm) **dried konbu** (kelp)

2 cups **water**

1 cup **dried bonito flakes**

½ cup **mirin**

⅓ cup **sodium-reduced soy sauce**

2 tbsp **granulated sugar**

1 tbsp **sake**

SOBA SAUCE: In saucepan, soak konbu in water for 15 minutes. Bring just to boil over medium heat. Remove konbu and discard.

Stir bonito flakes into konbu liquid; simmer for 6 minutes. Add mirin, soy sauce, sugar and sake; return to boil. Strain through cheesecloth-lined sieve into liquid measure; let cool completely.

Meanwhile, in saucepan of boiling water, cook noodles according to package directions. Drain and rinse under cold running water. Drain well; shake. Set aside to air-dry for 10 minutes.

Meanwhile, in covered skillet, steam spinach with ¼ cup water, stirring occasionally, just until wilted. Drain in colander; press out excess moisture.

Toss together noodles, spinach and about 1 cup of the soba sauce; divide among 4 bowls. Top with tofu; sprinkle with onions, nori (if using) and sesame seeds. Serve with remaining soba sauce, adding as desired and tossing to coat.

MAKES 4 SERVINGS. PER SERVING: about 369 cal, 20 g pro, 4 g total fat (1 g sat. fat), 64 g carb, 6 g fibre, 0 mg chol, 918 mg sodium, 725 mg potassium. % RDI: 22% calcium, 44% iron, 106% vit A, 18% vit C, 92% folate.

This delicious buckwheat noodle dish is a great vegetarian main course, but it also makes a nice side with Maple Soy–Glazed Salmon (opposite). Pea shoots are not as tender as pea tendrils, so they need to be cooked before eating.

SOBA NOODLES WITH PEA SHOOTS & SHIITAKES

1 pkg (8 oz/250 g) **soba noodles**

1 tbsp each **sesame oil** and **vegetable oil**

2 cloves **garlic,** minced

10 oz (280 g) **shiitake mushrooms,** stemmed and sliced

12 oz (340 g) **snow pea shoots** (about 8 cups)

⅓ cup **light mayonnaise**

¼ cup **sodium-reduced soy sauce**

1 tbsp **unseasoned rice vinegar**

1 tsp **granulated sugar .**

1 tsp **sambal oelek** or hot sauce (optional)

In saucepan of boiling water, cook noodles according to package directions. Drain and rinse under cold running water. Drain well; shake. Transfer to large bowl.

In wok or large skillet, heat half each of the sesame oil and vegetable oil over medium-high heat; sauté garlic until fragrant, about 15 seconds.

Add mushrooms; sauté until tender, about 4 minutes. Add to noodles.

In wok, heat remaining oils; stir-fry pea shoots until wilted and tender, about 5 minutes. Add to noodle mixture.

Whisk together mayonnaise, soy sauce, rice vinegar, sugar, and sambal oelek (if using); pour over noodle mixture, tossing to coat. Serve at room temperature or chilled.

TIP: Look for soba noodles in the sushi or Asian sections of health food stores and supermarkets.

MAKES 6 SERVINGS. PER SERVING: about 247 cal, 10 g pro, 10 g total fat (1 g sat. fat), 34 g carb, 4 g fibre, 5 mg chol, 523 mg sodium, 186 mg potassium. % RDI: 1% calcium, 8% iron, 21% vit A, 47% vit C, 18% folate.

A little salty, with just a touch of heat, this salmon is wonderful with Soba Noodles With Pea Shoots & Shiitakes (opposite). All you need is a quick broil at the end to give the fish a golden, glazed finish. This recipe doubles easily for a stress-free dinner party.

MAPLE SOY-GLAZED SALMON

4 **salmon fillets** (about 6 oz/170 g each)

¼ cup **maple syrup**

2 tsp **sodium-reduced soy sauce**

2 tsp **lime juice**

1 **jalapeño pepper,** seeded and minced

1 small clove **garlic,** minced

Pinch **pepper**

Place salmon in shallow dish. Stir together maple syrup, soy sauce, lime juice, jalapeño pepper, garlic and pepper; pour half over salmon and turn to coat. Cover and refrigerate for 30 minutes, turning once.

Place salmon on foil-lined baking sheet. Roast in 450°F (230°C) oven, brushing halfway through with remaining marinade, until fish flakes easily when tested, about 10 minutes. Broil until glazed, about 3 minutes.

MAKES 4 SERVINGS. PER SERVING: about 330 cal, 30 g pro, 17 g total fat (3 g sat. fat), 14 g carb, trace fibre, 84 mg chol, 172 mg sodium. % RDI: 3% calcium, 6% iron, 2% vit A, 12% vit C, 21% folate.

Sliced diagonally to reveal a colourful filling, these wraps make an elegant luncheon entrée. They can also be cut into 1½-inch (4 cm) thick slices and served as hors d'oeuvres.

BUCKWHEAT CHIVE CRÊPES WITH SMOKED SALMON

2 pkg (4½ oz/130 g each) **goat cheese,** softened

2 tbsp chopped **fresh dill** or fresh chives

2 tsp grated **lemon zest**

2 tsp **lemon juice**

¼ tsp each **salt** and **pepper**

2 pkg (5 oz/150 g each) **sliced smoked salmon** (about 24 slices)

4 cups **mixed baby greens**

BUCKWHEAT CHIVE CRÊPES:

⅔ cup **all-purpose flour**

⅔ cup **dark buckwheat flour**

¼ tsp **salt**

4 **eggs**

1½ cups **milk**

¼ cup **butter,** melted

3 tbsp finely chopped **fresh chives**

BUCKWHEAT CHIVE CRÊPES: In bowl, whisk together all-purpose flour, buckwheat flour and salt. Whisk together eggs, milk and 2 tbsp of the butter; pour over dry ingredients and whisk until smooth. Strain through fine sieve into bowl. Cover and refrigerate for 1 hour. (*Make-ahead: Refrigerate for up to 24 hours.*)

Lightly brush 8-inch (20 cm) crêpe pan or skillet with some of the remaining butter; heat over medium heat. Stir chives into batter.

Using scant ¼ cup for each crêpe, pour batter into centre of pan, swirling pan to coat; cook, turning once, until golden, about 1 minute. Transfer to plate.

Repeat with remaining batter, brushing skillet with some of the remaining butter as needed between batches. (*Make-ahead: Layer between waxed paper and wrap in plastic wrap; refrigerate for up to 3 days or freeze in airtight container for up to 1 month.*)

Blend together goat cheese, dill, lemon zest, lemon juice, salt and pepper; spread rounded 1 tbsp over each crêpe.

Lay 1½ slices salmon in line along centre of each crêpe; top with ¼ cup of the mixed greens. Roll up tightly and place, seam side down, on plate. (*Make-ahead: Cover and refrigerate for up to 24 hours.*)

To serve, cut in half on diagonal.

MAKES 8 SERVINGS. PER SERVING: about 316 cal, 20 g pro, 18 g total fat (10 g sat. fat), 19 g carb, 2 g fibre, 135 mg chol, 639 mg sodium, 329 mg potassium. % RDI: 13% calcium, 17% iron, 28% vit A, 8% vit C, 30% folate.

Tonkatsu sauce, a Japanese sauce often eaten with *tonkatsu* (pork cutlets), is available in the Asian sections of some grocery stores and at most Asian markets. It's also easy to make (see recipe, below right), and leftover sauce keeps in the fridge for up to a month.

WHOLE GRAIN PORK TENDERLOIN YAKISOBA

1 pkg (8 oz/250 g) **soba noodles**

8 oz (225 g) **pork tenderloin**

1 tbsp **sesame oil**

1 **carrot**

Half **sweet green pepper**

1 tbsp **vegetable oil**

2 cups thinly shredded **cabbage**

½ cup **bean sprouts**

⅓ cup **tonkatsu sauce**

2 tbsp **pickled shredded ginger**

2 tbsp **shredded nori** or
   thinly sliced green onions

✳ *TIP:* Nori is blackish green dried laver seaweed that's wrapped around sushi rolls. It is toasted and sold in large sheets, in strips or shredded at Asian grocery stores and some supermarkets. If you buy sheets or strips of nori, you can easily shred them with a knife or kitchen scissors.

In saucepan of boiling water, cook noodles according to package directions. Drain and rinse under cold running water. Drain well; shake. Set aside.

Meanwhile, cut pork lengthwise into 3 strips; cut crosswise into thin slices. Toss pork with sesame oil; set aside.

Cut carrot in half lengthwise; thinly slice. Thinly slice green pepper.

In wok or large skillet, heat vegetable oil over high heat; stir-fry pork mixture until browned, about 1 minute. Add cabbage, carrot and green pepper; stir-fry until vegetables are tender-crisp, about 2 minutes.

Add soba noodles, bean sprouts, tonkatsu sauce and ginger; toss together until hot and well combined. Scrape onto serving platter; sprinkle with nori.

MAKE YOUR OWN
Tonkatsu Sauce
In saucepan, mix 1 cup ketchup, ½ cup Worcestershire sauce, ½ cup sake or chicken broth, ¼ cup granulated sugar, ¼ cup mirin (or 2 tbsp corn syrup) and 2 tbsp each minced fresh ginger and garlic. Bring to boil. Reduce heat to medium and simmer until reduced by half, 20 minutes. *(Make-ahead: Transfer to airtight container; refrigerate for up to 1 month.)*

MAKES 1⅓ CUPS.

MAKES 3 OR 4 SERVINGS. PER EACH OF 4 SERVINGS: about 386 cal, 24 g pro, 8 g total fat (1 g sat. fat), 58 g carb, 4 g fibre, 31 mg chol, 455 mg sodium, 514 mg potassium. % RDI: 4% calcium, 17% iron, 36% vit A, 40% vit C, 18% folate.

This salad can be a fabulous gluten-free option – just be sure to use homemade vegetable stock instead of commercial broth, and check the labels on your curry paste, yogurt and chutney to make sure they're gluten-free.

CURRIED KASHA SALAD

1¾ cups **kasha**

3½ cups hot **vegetable broth**

4 tsp **curry paste**

1 tbsp minced **fresh ginger**

1 cup chopped **fresh mint** or fresh parsley

¼ cup **lemon juice**

2 tbsp **vegetable oil**

3 **green onions,** chopped

2 cloves **garlic,** minced

Pinch **salt**

1 piece (6 inches/15 cm) **cucumber,** diced

¼ cup chopped **almonds,** toasted

TOPPING:

½ cup **plain yogurt**

1 tbsp strained **mango chutney**

In dry saucepan, cook kasha over high heat, stirring, until fragrant, about 2 minutes.

Add broth, curry paste and ginger; reduce heat, cover and cook until no liquid remains, about 15 minutes. Let cool; fluff with fork.

In large bowl, whisk together mint, lemon juice, oil, green onions, garlic and salt. Add kasha, cucumber and almonds; toss to coat.

TOPPING: Whisk yogurt with chutney. *(Make-ahead: Refrigerate salad and topping in separate airtight containers for up to 24 hours.)* Serve on salad.

MAKES 4 TO 6 SERVINGS. PER EACH OF 6 SERVINGS: about 297 cal, 9 g pro, 11 g total fat (1 g sat. fat), 45 g carb, 7 g fibre, 2 mg chol, 452 mg sodium. % RDI: 8% calcium, 21% iron, 5% vit A, 13% vit C, 22% folate.

Orange zest and juice give this grilled chicken a bright flavour that enhances the gentle blend of spices. It's tasty with flavourful Curried Kasha Salad (opposite) or other whole grain salads. Because the chicken is cut in half before it's placed on the barbecue, it cooks more quickly than a whole chicken.

SPICY ORANGE PAPRIKA GRILLED CHICKEN

3 lb (1.35 kg) **whole chicken,** cut in half

1 tbsp grated **orange zest**

1 tbsp **orange juice**

1 tbsp **extra-virgin olive oil**

1 tbsp **liquid honey**

2 tsp **sweet paprika**

1 tsp each **ground coriander** and **ground ginger**

¾ tsp **salt**

½ tsp **cayenne pepper**

2 small cloves **garlic,** minced

Place chicken in shallow dish. Whisk together orange zest, orange juice, oil, honey, paprika, coriander, ginger, salt, cayenne and garlic; brush over chicken. Cover and refrigerate for 10 minutes. (*Make-ahead: Refrigerate for up to 24 hours.*)

Heat 1 burner of 2-burner barbecue or 2 outside burners of 3-burner barbecue. Brush grill over unlit burner with oil.

Place chicken, bone side down, on greased grill. Close lid and grill, turning once, until juices run clear when thigh is pierced, about 45 minutes.

Move any pieces that need more crisping (without overbrowning) over direct heat. Transfer to cutting board. Let stand for 10 minutes before carving.

MAKES 4 SERVINGS. PER SERVING (WITHOUT SKIN): about 277 cal, 29 g pro, 15 g total fat (4 g sat. fat), 7 g carb, 1 g fibre, 102 mg chol, 520 mg sodium, 388 mg potassium. % RDI: 2% calcium, 11% iron, 10% vit A, 8% vit C, 5% folate.

Kasha mixed with bow tie pasta is a classic European side dish, often served under the name *kasha varnishkes*. It's often served on holiday tables and as part of celebratory menus.

BOW TIE PASTA WITH KASHA

12 oz (340 g) **bow tie pasta**

1 tbsp **olive oil**

1 cup **kasha**

1 **egg white**

1 tbsp **butter**

2 cups **sodium-reduced chicken broth**

5 **shallots,** thinly sliced

½ cup **sour cream**

½ cup **whipping cream** (35%)

1 tbsp **Dijon mustard**

¾ cup chopped **fresh dill**

¾ tsp **salt**

½ tsp freshly ground **pepper**

In large pot of boiling salted water, cook pasta until al dente, about 10 minutes. Reserving ½ cup of the cooking liquid, drain. In large bowl, toss pasta with olive oil. Set aside.

Meanwhile, stir kasha with egg white until well coated. In deep 12-inch (30 cm) skillet, melt butter over medium-high heat; toast kasha, stirring constantly, until dry and fragrant, about 5 minutes. Add broth and shallots; cook just until kasha is tender, 12 to 14 minutes.

Reduce heat to low. Stir in sour cream, whipping cream, mustard, pasta and reserved cooking liquid; toss until pasta is well coated. Stir in dill, salt and pepper.

MAKES 4 TO 6 SERVINGS. PER EACH OF 6 SERVINGS: about 452 cal, 14 g pro, 16 g total fat (8 g sat. fat), 66 g carb, 6 g fibre, 38 mg chol, 741 mg sodium, 226 mg potassium. % RDI: 6% calcium, 23% iron, 12% vit A, 2% vit C, 61% folate.

This dish is cooked like a traditional pilaf, with one exception: The kasha kernels are mixed with egg white before you toast them and add the broth. This keeps them from getting sticky and breaking apart as they cook.

KASHA PILAF WITH SWEET POTATO & KALE

2 tbsp **olive oil**

1 large **sweet potato,** peeled and cut in ½-inch (1 cm) chunks

2¼ cups **chicken broth**

6 cups coarsely chopped **kale**

4 cloves **garlic,** minced

½ tsp **salt**

1 small **onion,** finely chopped

½ tsp **five-spice powder**

½ tsp **medium curry paste**

1 cup **kasha**

1 **egg white**

1 tbsp **butter**

In large skillet, heat 1 tbsp of the oil over medium-high heat; sauté sweet potato until starting to soften, about 4 minutes. Cover, reduce heat to low and cook until tender-crisp, about 4 minutes.

Add 2 tbsp of the chicken broth to pan; cook, scraping up browned bits. Stir in kale, 1 tsp of the garlic and ¼ tsp of the salt. Cover and cook until kale is wilted and tender, about 5 minutes. Remove from heat; keep warm.

Meanwhile, in separate skillet, heat remaining oil over medium-high heat; sauté onion until softened and starting to brown, 4 minutes.

Add remaining garlic and salt, five-spice powder and curry paste; cook, stirring, until fragrant, about 1 minute. Transfer to bowl; set aside. Wipe out skillet.

Stir kasha with egg white until well coated. In skillet, melt butter over medium heat; toast kasha, stirring constantly, until dry and fragrant, about 5 minutes.

Add onion mixture and remaining broth to kasha; cook, scraping up browned bits. Bring to simmer, stirring occasionally; simmer until liquid is absorbed and kasha is tender but still firm, about 15 minutes.

Cover and let stand for 2 minutes. Stir in sweet potato mixture.

MAKES 4 TO 6 SERVINGS. PER EACH OF 6 SERVINGS: about 241 cal, 8 g pro, 8 g total fat (2 g sat. fat), 38 g carb, 6 g fibre, 5 mg chol, 483 mg sodium, 540 mg potassium. % RDI: 11% calcium, 18% iron, 173% vit A, 125% vit C, 16% folate.

These wholesome muffins have a soft jam filling and a crunchy orange-almond topping. They're heavenly warm out of the pan, but the jam helps keep them moist if you wait a day to eat them. Stir quick breads like this just until the dry ingredients are moistened – no more – to ensure a light, tender texture.

STREUSEL-TOPPED BUCKWHEAT & FIG JAM MUFFINS

1 cup **rolled buckwheat flakes**

¾ cup **all-purpose flour**

½ cup **dark buckwheat flour**

½ cup packed **brown sugar**

1 tsp **baking soda**

1 tsp **baking powder**

¾ tsp **salt**

¾ cup **milk**

½ cup **sour cream**

6 tbsp **butter,** melted

1 **egg**

2 tbsp **liquid honey**

2 tsp grated **orange zest**

5 tbsp **fig jam** or apricot jam

ORANGE-ALMOND STREUSEL:

½ cup **all-purpose flour**

¼ cup **granulated sugar**

¼ cup finely chopped **almonds**

2 tbsp grated **orange zest**

¼ cup **butter,** melted

ORANGE-ALMOND STREUSEL:
In bowl, whisk together flour, sugar, almonds and orange zest. With fingers or fork, blend in butter until mixture resembles wet sand. Set aside.

In large bowl, whisk together buckwheat flakes, all-purpose and buckwheat flours, brown sugar, baking soda, baking powder and salt. Whisk together milk, sour cream, butter, egg, honey and orange zest. Pour over flour mixture and stir just until dry ingredients are moistened.

Spoon half of the batter into 12 greased or paper-lined muffin cups. Spoon heaping 1 tsp of the jam into centre of each muffin cup; top with remaining batter. Sprinkle with streusel.

Bake in 375°F (190°C) oven until tops are golden and firm to the touch, 17 to 20 minutes.

Let cool in pan on rack for 2 minutes. Transfer to rack; let cool. (*Make-ahead: Store in airtight container for up to 24 hours.*)

MAKES 12 MUFFINS. PER MUFFIN: about 302 cal, 5 g pro, 13 g total fat (7 g sat. fat), 42 g carb, 2 g fibre, 46 mg chol, 365 mg sodium, 146 mg potassium. % RDI: 6% calcium, 10% iron, 11% vit A, 5% vit C, 15% folate.

Clockwise from top left:
Kasha, unroasted buckwheat
groats, soba noodles and
rolled buckwheat flakes

BUCKWHEAT

WHY IT'S GOOD FOR YOU: Buckwheat is a seed, not a grain, so it's a gluten-free option for people with celiac disease or gluten intolerance. It is a source of protein and is rich in phytochemicals. Buckwheat is also a good source of magnesium, and it contains B vitamins, iron and zinc, in addition to some fibre.

WHOLE GRAIN FORMS: Uncooked whole buckwheat kernels are called **groats.** When these groats are roasted, they are often sold under the name **kasha. Rolled flakes** have been rolled to flatten them, which makes them cook quickly. They are similar to rolled oats and can be used in the same way. **Soba noodles** are Japanese dried noodles made from buckwheat flour. Check the label: Many brands contain a mix of whole grain and refined flours, but there are 100 per cent whole grain versions available. **Whole grain flour** is made by grinding unroasted buckwheat groats; this is called dark buckwheat flour (light doesn't contain the germ and bran). It's gluten-free, so risen baked goods often mix buckwheat with other flours.

STORAGE: Buckwheat noodles are shelf stable. Store rolled flakes and kasha in airtight containers at room temperature for up to six months. Freeze buckwheat flour for up to six months.

USES: Buckwheat flakes are tasty in granola and porridge. Try soba noodles in Asian-style soups and stir-fries. Kasha has a strong flavour, so it's best in well-spiced dishes. Buckwheat flour is great for pancakes – especially blinis – and baked goods.

Natural (wheat) bran consists of the hard outer layer of the wheat kernel and is an excellent source of insoluble fibre, which is great for digestion. These gems are an appetizing way to boost your fibre intake first thing in the morning.

RYE BRAN MUFFINS

1¼ cups **dark rye flour**

½ cup **whole wheat flour**

½ cup **natural bran**

1¼ tsp **baking powder**

¾ tsp **salt**

½ tsp **baking soda**

1 **egg**

1¼ cups **buttermilk**

⅓ cup **vegetable oil**

¼ cup **liquid honey**

2 tbsp **fancy molasses**

¾ cup chopped **walnuts**

¾ cup **dried currants**

¼ cup **large-flake rolled oats**

In large bowl, whisk together rye and wheat flours, bran, baking powder, salt and baking soda.

Whisk together egg, buttermilk, oil, honey and molasses; pour over flour mixture. Sprinkle with walnuts and currants; stir just until combined.

Spoon into 10 greased or paper-lined muffin cups. Sprinkle with oats. Bake in 375°F (190°C) oven until cake tester inserted in centre of several muffins comes out clean, about 22 minutes.

Let cool in pan on rack for 2 minutes. Transfer to rack; let cool. *(Make-ahead: Wrap separately in plastic wrap and freeze in airtight container for up to 2 weeks.)*

MAKES 10 MUFFINS. PER MUFFIN: about 305 cal, 8 g pro, 15 g total fat (2 g sat. fat), 41 g carb, 6 g fibre, 20 mg chol, 305 mg sodium. % RDI: 9% calcium, 19% iron, 1% vit A, 2% vit C, 11% folate.

These festive loaves, inspired by rich holiday breads from Alsace, are delicious sliced thinly and served with cheese. They require a lot of ingredients and three rises, but they're definitely worth the work.

WHOLE GRAIN FRUIT & NUT BREAD

¾ cup **boiling water**

½ cup each chopped **dried pears, dried apples** and **dried figs**

¼ cup **raisins**

¼ cup **candied mixed peel**

¼ cup **kirsch**

¼ cup each chopped **hazelnuts** and **almonds,** toasted

1½ tsp **cinnamon**

½ tsp **ground star anise**

¼ tsp **ground cloves**

Pinch each **nutmeg** and **pepper**

¼ cup **granulated sugar**

½ tsp **salt**

1 pkg (8 g) **active dry yeast** (2¼ tsp)

3½ cups **whole wheat bread flour** (approx)

2 cups **dark rye flour**

SUGAR SYRUP:
⅓ cup each **granulated sugar** and **water**

1 tbsp **kirsch**

In bowl, combine boiling water, pears, apples, figs, raisins, peel and kirsch. Cover; let stand for 1 hour. Reserving liquid, drain. Into fruit, stir hazelnuts, almonds, cinnamon, anise, cloves, nutmeg and pepper.

Add water to liquid to make 2 cups. In saucepan, heat liquid, sugar and salt over medium heat until sugar is dissolved. Transfer to bowl; let cool to lukewarm. Sprinkle in yeast; let stand until frothy, 10 minutes. Stir in 2 cups of the wheat flour and rye flour to make sticky dough.

On floured surface, knead, adding remaining flour as needed to prevent sticking, until smooth and elastic, 10 minutes. Place in greased bowl; turn to grease all over. Cover; let rise in warm place until doubled in bulk, 2 hours. Toss fruit with ¼ cup of the remaining flour.

Punch down dough. On floured surface, knead in fruit; shape into ball. Place in greased bowl. Cover; refrigerate for 8 hours or overnight.

Halve dough. Roll each into 11- x 8-inch (28 x 20 cm) rectangle. From narrow end, roll up each into cylinder; pinch seams to seal. Fit, seam side down, into 2 greased 8- x 4-inch (1.5 L) loaf pans. Cover; let rise until doubled, 1½ to 2 hours. Cut ¼-inch (5 mm) deep slit along tops. Bake in 400°F (200°C) oven for 20 minutes. Reduce heat to 350°F (180°C); bake until dark golden and bottoms sound hollow when tapped, 30 minutes.

SUGAR SYRUP: In saucepan, boil sugar with water until reduced to ¼ cup, 3 to 5 minutes. Stir in kirsch; brush over warm loaves. Remove from pans; let cool on racks.

MAKES 2 LOAVES, 12 SLICES EACH. PER SLICE: about 175 cal, 5 g pro, 2 g total fat (trace sat. fat), 37 g carb, 6 g fibre, 0 mg chol, 56 mg sodium, 262 mg potassium. % RDI: 3% calcium, 14% iron, 2% vit C, 9% folate.

There's nothing quite as delicious as a slice of fresh pumpernickel bread – as toast, in a sandwich or spread with lashings of butter. If you're not a fan of caraway seeds, just omit them.

PUMPERNICKEL BREAD

Pinch **granulated sugar**

¼ cup warm **water**

1 pkg (8 g) **active dry yeast** (2¼ tsp)

2 tbsp **unsalted butter**

2 tbsp **cider vinegar**

2 tbsp **blackstrap molasses**

½ oz (15 g) **unsweetened chocolate,** chopped

2 cups **all-purpose flour** (approx)

1½ cups **dark rye flour**

½ cup **oat bran**

1 tbsp **caraway seeds** (approx)

1½ tsp **instant espresso powder**

1½ tsp **salt**

1 **egg**

In bowl, dissolve sugar in warm water; sprinkle yeast over top. Let stand until frothy, 10 minutes.

Meanwhile, in small saucepan, stir together 1 cup water, butter, vinegar, molasses and chocolate; cook, stirring, over medium heat until chocolate is melted and smooth, about 5 minutes. Let cool.

In large bowl, whisk together 1¾ cups of the all-purpose flour, rye flour, oat bran, 1 tbsp of the caraway seeds, espresso powder and salt. Stir in yeast and chocolate mixtures until dough comes together and pulls away from side of bowl.

Turn dough out onto lightly floured surface; knead, adding as much of the remaining all-purpose flour as needed to prevent sticking, until smooth and elastic, 10 minutes.

Place dough in greased bowl; turn to grease all over. Cover and let rise in warm draft-free place until doubled in bulk, about 1½ hours.

Lightly push down dough. Turn out onto lightly floured surface; pat into 8-inch (20 cm) square. Roll up into cylinder; pinch seam to seal. Place, seam side down, in 8- x 4-inch (1.5 L) loaf pan. Cover and let rise in warm, draft-free place until doubled in bulk, 1½ hours.

Whisk egg with 1 tbsp water; brush over loaf. Sprinkle with pinch caraway seeds. Bake in 350°F (180°C) oven until instant-read thermometer inserted in centre registers 200°F (93°C) or loaf sounds hollow when tapped, about 40 minutes. Transfer loaf to rack; let cool.

MAKES 1 LOAF, OR 12 SLICES. PER SLICE: about 179 cal, 6 g pro, 4 g total fat (2 g sat. fat), 33 g carb, 4 g fibre, 21 mg chol, 296 mg sodium, 293 mg potassium. % RDI: 5% calcium, 24% iron, 2% vit A, 31% folate.

This lighter version of rye bread makes terrific sandwiches. Try it on a Reuben (pictured, left) or with corned beef or pastrami for an old-fashioned deli-style lunch.

LIGHT CARAWAY RYE BREAD

1 tbsp **fancy molasses**

½ cup warm **water**

1 pkg (8 g) **active dry yeast** (2¼ tsp)

2¾ cups **white bread flour**

1¾ cups **dark rye flour**

2 tsp **caraway seeds**

1 tsp **salt**

1¼ cups **buttermilk**

In bowl, dissolve molasses in warm water; sprinkle yeast over top. Let stand until frothy, 10 minutes. Meanwhile, in large bowl, whisk together 2½ cups of the bread flour, rye flour, caraway seeds and salt. Stir in yeast mixture and buttermilk to make sticky dough.

Turn dough out onto lightly floured surface; knead, adding as much of the remaining bread flour as needed to prevent sticking, until smooth and elastic, 10 minutes.

Place dough in greased bowl; turn to grease all over. Cover and let rise in warm draft-free place until doubled in bulk, about 1½ hours.

Lightly push down dough. Turn out onto lightly floured surface; pat into 9-inch (23 cm) square. Roll up into cylinder; pinch seam to seal.

Place, seam side down, in 9- x 5-inch (2 L) loaf pan. Cover and let rise in warm draft-free place until doubled in bulk, about 1½ hours.

Bake in 350°F (180°C) oven until instant-read thermometer inserted in centre registers 200°F (93°C) or loaf sounds hollow when tapped, about 40 minutes. Transfer loaf to rack; let cool.

CHANGE IT UP
Bread Machine Light Caraway Rye Bread
Substitute bread machine yeast for active dry yeast. Into pan of bread machine, place, in order: buttermilk, warm water, molasses, salt, caraway seeds, white flour, rye flour and yeast. Use Whole Grain setting.

MAKES 1 LOAF, OR 12 SLICES. PER SLICE: about 189 cal, 7 g pro, 1 g total fat (trace sat. fat), 37 g carb, 3 g fibre, 2 mg chol, 215 mg sodium, 173 mg potassium. % RDI: 5% calcium, 14% iron, 25% folate.

This soft, fairly dense yeast-risen loaf requires no starter and minimal rising time. Barley malt syrup is the tastiest for bread baking; wheat malt syrup is milder and sweeter. Either is balanced nicely by the tart yogurt. Look for malt syrup at health food, bulk food and large grocery stores.

MALT & YOGURT RYE BREAD

¼ tsp **granulated sugar**

¾ cup warm **water**

2½ tsp **active dry yeast**

1 cup **nonfat yogurt**

¼ cup **malt syrup**

1½ tsp **salt**

2⅓ cups **dark rye flour**

2 cups **white bread flour** (approx)

1½ tsp **butter,** melted

2 tsp **caraway seeds**

In large bowl, dissolve sugar in warm water; sprinkle in yeast. Let stand until frothy, 10 minutes. Stir in yogurt, malt syrup and salt until combined. Stir in rye flour and bread flour to make shaggy dough.

Turn out onto floured surface; knead, adding up to ½ cup more bread flour as needed, until smooth and elastic, about 10 minutes. Place in greased bowl; turn to grease all over. Cover; let rise in warm place until doubled in bulk, 1½ hours.

Gently press down dough. On floured surface, knead lightly; shape into ball, stretching and pinching underneath to smooth top. Cover; let rest for 10 minutes. Flatten into 1-inch (2.5 cm) thick oval. Starting at long side, fold top and bottom thirds over centre to form torpedo-shaped loaf; pinch seam to seal.

Place, seam side down, on parchment paper–lined baking sheet. Cover and let rise in warm place until doubled in bulk, ¾ to 1¼ hours.

Brush top with butter; sprinkle with caraway seeds. With serrated knife, cut three or four ½-inch (1 cm) deep slits in top of loaf.

Place pan in 425°F (220°C) oven; spritz walls and floor with cold water (avoiding lightbulb) until steam fills oven, about 10 seconds. Quickly close door to trap steam. Bake for 20 minutes, repeating steaming after 3 minutes.

Reduce heat to 375°F (190°C); bake until crust is hard and loaf sounds hollow when tapped on bottom, about 25 minutes. Transfer to rack; let cool.

MAKES 1 LOAF, OR 16 TO 20 SLICES. PER EACH OF 20 SLICES: about 115 cal, 5 g pro, 1 g total fat (trace sat. fat), 23 g carb, 3 g fibre, 1 mg chol, 184 mg sodium, 170 mg potassium. % RDI: 3% calcium, 12% iron, 15% folate.

Clockwise from top left: Dark rye flour, rolled rye flakes and rye berries

PROFILE:

RYE

WHY IT'S GOOD FOR YOU: Rye is a nutritional powerhouse that's been used in Europe for centuries. High in fibre, it's an excellent source of manganese. Rye is also a good source of selenium and magnesium, and contains B vitamins, phosphorus, iron and zinc.

WHOLE GRAIN FORMS: Rye **berries** are the dried whole unrefined kernels of the plant. **Rolled flakes** are made by steaming and rolling rye berries. They are similar to rolled oats and can be used in many of the same ways. **Whole grain flour** is ground from whole rye berries and is a common sight in supermarkets. It's available in light and dark varieties; dark contains the bran and germ, making it a whole grain choice. Light rye flour does not contain the bran and germ, and is not considered a whole grain ingredient. Stone-ground dark rye flour is the purest whole grain form.

STORAGE: Rye contains natural oils that can go rancid. For best results, freeze dark rye flour and rye berries in airtight containers for up to six months. Rye flakes are fine in the pantry, but seal packages tightly and use within two months.

USES: Dark rye flour makes delicious breads, crackers and other baked goods. Try rye flakes in granola, porridge and crumble toppings. Rye berries are chewy and tasty in grain salads or other dishes in which wheat berries are often used.

Serve this molasses-rich steamed bread with baked beans for a traditional East Coast dinner. It's also delicious toasted and spread with butter – or on its own right out of the can. If you'd like, you can add ¾ cup raisins, chopped dates or chopped dried apricots to the dough.

MARITIME BROWN BREAD

1 cup **whole wheat flour**

1 cup **dark rye flour**

1 cup **fine stone-ground cornmeal**

1½ tsp **baking soda**

1 tsp **salt**

1½ cups **buttermilk,** at room temperature

¾ cup **fancy molasses**

½ cup **unsweetened applesauce**

Grease two clean 28-oz (796 mL) tomato cans. Grease two 8-inch (20 cm) squares of parchment paper or foil; set aside.

In large bowl, whisk together whole wheat flour, rye flour, cornmeal, baking soda and salt. Whisk together buttermilk, molasses and applesauce; pour over flour mixture and stir just until blended.

Divide dough between prepared cans. Cover cans with prepared paper, greased side down and leaving 1-inch (2.5 cm) space inside for bread to rise above rim of can; tie securely with kitchen string.

Place cans on steamer rack or heatproof trivet in deep pot or Dutch oven just large enough to accommodate width of cans. Pour in enough boiling water to come halfway up sides of cans.

Cover and return to boil over medium heat; reduce heat and simmer, adding more boiling water if necessary to maintain level, until cake tester inserted in centre comes out clean, about 2½ hours.

Remove from cans; let cool on racks. (Make-ahead: Wrap in plastic wrap and store for up to 5 days.)

MAKES 2 LOAVES, ABOUT 10 SLICES EACH. PER SLICE: about 109 cal, 3 g pro, 1 g total fat (trace sat. fat), 24 g carb, 2 g fibre, 1 mg chol, 227 mg sodium. % RDI: 5% calcium, 9% iron, 2% vit C, 4% folate.

These gluten-free crackers couldn't be simpler to make. Their toasted garlic-and-onion flavour is excellent with spreads, such as Roasted Vegetable Hummus (page 157), but they're also just as delicious on their own. Look for dehydrated minced garlic in the spice aisle.

ONION & GARLIC BUCKWHEAT CRACKERS

½ cup **brown rice flour**

¼ cup **dark buckwheat flour**

¼ cup **ground flaxseeds**

2 tbsp **cornstarch**

¼ tsp **salt**

2 tbsp **olive oil**

¼ cup **vegetable broth** (approx)

TOPPING:

1 tsp **dehydrated minced garlic**

½ tsp **onion powder**

¼ tsp **salt**

¼ tsp **poppy seeds**

½ tsp **olive oil**

TIP: Shaping the dough into a rectangle first makes it easier to maintain that shape as you roll it out.

In large bowl, whisk together brown rice flour, buckwheat flour, ground flaxseeds, cornstarch and salt. Stir in oil until mixture resembles bread crumbs. Gradually stir in broth, adding up to 1 tbsp more, 1 tsp at a time, if necessary, until soft but not sticky dough forms. Dough should hold together and not be crumbly.

Shape dough into rectangle. Between 2 sheets of parchment paper, roll out dough into ¹⁄₁₆-inch (1.5 mm) thick rectangle. Peel off top paper; with tip of sharp knife, score dough into 2-inch (5 cm) squares or 2- x 4-inch (5 x 10 cm) rectangles.

TOPPING: Mix together garlic, onion powder, salt and poppy seeds. Brush dough with oil; sprinkle with garlic mixture.

Slide parchment and dough onto large rimless baking sheet. Bake in 400°F (200°C) oven until crisp and sizzling, about 12 minutes.

Let cool on pan on rack; break along score lines. (*Make-ahead: Store in airtight container for up to 1 week.*)

MAKES THIRTY 2-INCH (5 CM) SQUARE CRACKERS. PER CRACKER: about 29 cal, 1 g pro, 2 g total fat (trace sat. fat), 4 g carb, 1 g fibre, 0 mg chol, 45 mg sodium, 23 mg potassium. % RDI: 1% iron, 1% folate.

This cracker bread, called lavash, tastes better and is a lot cheaper than the store-bought version. Use a clean coffee grinder or mini chopper to grind your own flaxseeds; 3 tbsp seeds will yield about ¼ cup ground. If you grind a little too much, just add the leftovers to your next smoothie.

WHOLE WHEAT & RYE CRACKER BREAD

¾ cup **dark rye flour**

¾ cup **whole wheat bread flour**

¼ cup **flaxseeds**

¼ cup **ground flaxseeds**

4 tsp **butter,** softened

½ tsp **baking powder**

½ tsp **salt**

½ cup **milk**

In large bowl, beat together rye and whole wheat flours, flaxseeds, ground flaxseeds, butter, baking powder and salt until crumbly. Mix in milk to make soft sticky dough, adding up to 3 tbsp water, 1 tbsp at a time, if necessary to make pliable.

Turn out dough onto lightly floured surface; knead just until smooth. Wrap in plastic wrap; let stand for 10 minutes.

Divide dough into quarters. On lightly floured surface, roll out, one-quarter at a time, into ⅛-inch (3 mm) thick 10-inch (25 cm) square. Place on ungreased rimless baking sheets.

Bake, 2 sheets at a time, in top and bottom thirds of 325°F (160°C) oven, rotating and switching pans halfway through, until golden and crisp, about 20 minutes.

Let cool on pan on rack; break into pieces. *(Make-ahead: Store in airtight container for up to 1 week or freeze for up to 1 month.)*

MAKES ABOUT 40 PIECES. PER PIECE: about 29 cal, 1 g pro, 1 g total fat (trace sat. fat), 4 g carb, 1 g fibre, 1 mg chol, 38 mg sodium. % RDI: 1% calcium, 2% iron, 1% vit A, 4% folate.

Roasting carrots, shallots and garlic brings out their natural sweetness for a hummus that is lovely paired with crisp Whole Wheat & Rye Cracker Bread (opposite) and Onion & Garlic Buckwheat Crackers (page 155). If you prefer a thinner dip, add a little more water.

ROASTED VEGETABLE HUMMUS

2 large **carrots,** chopped

4 **shallots,** quartered

4 cloves **garlic** (unpeeled)

¼ cup **extra-virgin olive oil**

1 cup drained rinsed **canned chickpeas**

¼ cup **tahini**

2 tbsp **lemon juice**

¼ tsp **salt**

On rimmed baking sheet, toss together carrots, shallots, garlic and 1 tbsp of the oil. Bake in 400°F (200°C) oven, stirring twice, until tender, 35 to 40 minutes. Let cool. Squeeze garlic from skins.

In food processor, finely chop roasted vegetables with garlic. Add chickpeas, remaining oil, tahini, lemon juice and salt; pulse until smooth. Add 3 tbsp water, 1 tbsp at a time, until spreadable. *(Make-ahead: Cover and refrigerate in airtight container for up to 2 days. Stir just before serving.)*

MAKES 2 CUPS. PER 1 TBSP: about 37 cal, 1 g pro, 3 g total fat (trace sat. fat), 3 g carb, 1 g fibre, 0 mg chol, 39 mg sodium. % RDI: 1% calcium, 2% iron, 10% vit A, 2% vit C, 3% folate.

QUINOA, CORN & MILLET

Treat your family to a taste of southern cooking for breakfast. Cheesy and creamy, this savoury cereal is great on its own or as a side dish with sausages and eggs.

CHEDDAR CORNMEAL PORRIDGE

2 cups **milk**

1 cup **fine stone-ground cornmeal**

¼ tsp each **salt** and **pepper**

½ cup shredded **old Cheddar cheese**

2 tbsp **butter**

In saucepan, bring milk and 2¾ cups water to boil. Gradually whisk in cornmeal, salt and pepper.

Reduce heat and simmer, uncovered and stirring often, until no longer gritty, about 10 minutes. Remove from heat.

Add Cheddar cheese and butter; stir until melted.

TIP: You can substitute medium stone-ground cornmeal for the fine; just increase cooking time to 50 minutes.

MAKES 4 SERVINGS. PER SERVING: about 295 cal, 11 g pro, 13 g total fat (8 g sat. fat), 33 g carb, 3 g fibre, 40 mg chol, 326 mg sodium. % RDI: 23% calcium, 4% iron, 16% vit A, 32% folate.

These pancakes are light, fluffy and hearty all at once. If corn is in season, roast, grill or boil the cobs until tender-crisp and cut the kernels off instead of using frozen corn; the fresh, sweet flavour is worth the effort. Top these pancakes with butter and maple syrup, or try a spoonful of Cinnamon Fruit Compote (page 223).

SWEET CORN WHOLE WHEAT PANCAKES

1 cup **whole wheat flour**

¼ cup **fine stone-ground cornmeal**

1 tbsp **granulated sugar**

1 tsp **baking powder**

½ tsp **baking soda**

Pinch **salt**

1 **egg**

1¼ cups **buttermilk**

¼ cup **butter,** melted

1 cup **frozen corn kernels**

TIP: If you can only find medium-grind cornmeal, you can grind it finely at home. In food processor, whirl cornmeal until finely ground with a few larger grains remaining, 3 to 5 minutes.

In large bowl, whisk together whole wheat flour, cornmeal, sugar, baking powder, baking soda and salt. Whisk together egg, buttermilk and 2 tbsp of the butter; pour over flour mixture. Sprinkle with corn; stir just until combined.

Lightly brush large nonstick skillet with some of the remaining butter; heat over medium-high heat. Using ¼ cup for each pancake, pour in batter, spreading with spatula to 4-inch (10 cm) diameter. Cook until underside is golden and bubbles break on top that do not fill in, 3 to 4 minutes.

Turn pancakes; cook until underside is golden, 1 to 2 minutes.

Repeat with remaining batter, brushing skillet with some of the remaining butter as needed between batches. *(Make-ahead: Let cool. Stack pancakes, separated by waxed paper, and freeze in resealable freezer bag for up to 2 weeks. Reheat in toaster.)*

MAKES 10 PANCAKES. PER PANCAKE: about 135 cal, 4 g pro, 6 g total fat (4 g sat. fat), 17 g carb, 2 g fibre, 33 mg chol, 159 mg sodium, 158 mg potassium. % RDI: 6% calcium, 5% iron, 6% vit A, 2% vit C, 6% folate.

A tender, cheese-flavoured corn topping gives plain old chili a delicious lift. Fresh and frozen corn work equally well in this dish, so use whichever is on hand.

CHUNKY CHILI CORN BREAD COBBLER

2 lb (900 g) **beef outside round oven roast**

2 tbsp **vegetable oil**

1 **onion,** chopped

2 cloves **garlic,** minced

1 each rib **celery** and **carrot,** diced

2 tbsp **chili powder**

1 tsp **dried oregano**

¼ tsp **pepper**

1 can (19 oz/540 mL) **stewed tomatoes with chili seasonings**

1 can (14 oz/398 mL) **tomato sauce**

1 can (19 oz/540 mL) **red kidney beans,** drained and rinsed

¼ cup chopped **fresh cilantro**

CORN BREAD COBBLER:

1 cup **all-purpose flour**

½ cup **fine stone-ground cornmeal**

2 tsp **baking powder**

½ tsp each **baking soda** and **salt**

1 cup **buttermilk**

2 tbsp **butter,** melted

1 **egg**

2 cups **corn kernels**

1 cup shredded **Cheddar cheese**

Cut beef into ½-inch (1 cm) cubes. In large shallow Dutch oven, heat oil over medium-high heat; brown beef cubes, in batches. With slotted spoon, transfer to bowl.

Add onion, garlic, celery, carrot, chili powder, oregano and pepper to pan; cook over medium heat, stirring, until onion is softened, about 5 minutes.

Return beef and any accumulated juices to pan. Stir in tomatoes, tomato sauce and beans; bring to boil. Reduce heat, cover and simmer until beef is tender, about 1½ hours.

Stir in cilantro. *(Make-ahead: Let cool for 30 minutes; transfer to airtight container. Refrigerate for up to 24 hours or freeze for up to 1 month. Thaw in refrigerator for 24 hours. Transfer to 13- x 9-inch/ 3 L baking dish; cover with foil and bake in 400°F/200°C oven until bubbly, about 30 minutes.)*

CORN BREAD COBBLER: In bowl, whisk together flour, cornmeal, baking powder, baking soda and salt. Whisk together buttermilk, butter and egg; pour over flour mixture. Sprinkle with corn; stir just until combined. Spoon, in 8 dollops, over chili. Sprinkle with cheese.

Bake in 400°F (200°C) oven until topping is golden and no longer doughy underneath, 30 to 35 minutes. Let stand for 10 minutes before serving.

MAKES 8 SERVINGS. PER SERVING: about 492 cal, 41 g pro, 15 g total fat (6 g sat. fat), 51 g carb, 8 g fibre, 97 mg chol, 1,171 mg sodium. % RDI: 22% calcium, 47% iron, 47% vit A, 27% vit C, 35% folate.

Another southern-style family favourite, this one-dish meal is terrific to bring to a potluck or serve as a casual supper when entertaining friends.

CHICKEN & WHOLE WHEAT CORNMEAL DUMPLINGS

3 lb (1.35 kg) **whole chicken**

1 tbsp **vegetable oil**

2 each **carrots** and ribs **celery,** cut in chunks

1 **onion,** chopped

2 cloves **garlic,** minced

1 cup **sodium-reduced chicken broth**

2 **bay leaves**

1 tsp **dried thyme**

½ tsp each **salt** and **pepper**

¼ tsp **dried marjoram**

2 **potatoes,** peeled and cut in 1-inch (2.5 cm) cubes

3 tbsp **all-purpose flour**

DUMPLINGS:

½ cup **whole wheat flour**

¼ cup each **all-purpose flour** and **fine stone-ground cornmeal**

1 tsp **baking powder**

¼ tsp **baking soda**

Pinch **salt**

2 tbsp cold **butter,** cubed

⅔ cup **buttermilk**

2 tbsp chopped **fresh parsley**

Cut chicken into 8 pieces. Remove skin and discard; set chicken aside.

In shallow Dutch oven, heat oil over medium heat; cook carrots, celery, onion and garlic, stirring occasionally, until onion is softened, about 5 minutes.

Add 1½ cups water, broth, bay leaves, thyme, salt, pepper and marjoram; bring to boil. Add chicken; reduce heat, cover and simmer for 20 minutes.

Add potatoes; cover and simmer for 5 minutes. Whisk flour with ⅓ cup cold water; whisk into broth mixture.

DUMPLINGS: Meanwhile, in bowl, whisk together whole wheat flour, all-purpose flour, cornmeal, baking powder, baking soda and salt. Using pastry blender or 2 knives, cut in butter until in coarse crumbs. Stir in buttermilk and parsley to make sticky spoonable dough.

Spoon dough, in 8 dollops, over simmering stew. Cook, covered and without lifting lid, until dumplings are no longer doughy underneath and juices run clear when chicken is pierced, about 15 minutes. Discard bay leaves.

MAKES 6 TO 8 SERVINGS. PER EACH OF 8 SERVINGS: about 227 cal, 20 g pro, 7 g total fat (3 g sat. fat), 22 g carb, 3 g fibre, 59 mg chol, 339 mg sodium, 460 mg potassium. % RDI: 6% calcium, 11% iron, 30% vit A, 10% vit C, 12% folate.

Make polenta special by mixing in fresh corn, then grilling it and topping it with sweet and smoky roasted peppers. Two squares make a nice light vegetarian main dish, but you can serve the squares individually as appetizers if you like.

GRILLED CORN POLENTA WITH ROASTED RED PEPPERS

¾ tsp **salt**

1 cup **fine stone-ground cornmeal**

1 cup **fresh corn kernels**

½ cup grated **Parmesan cheese**

ROASTED RED PEPPERS:
3 **sweet red peppers**

1 tbsp **extra-virgin olive oil**

1 tsp **white wine vinegar**

Pinch **salt**

8 leaves **fresh basil,** thinly sliced

ROASTED RED PEPPERS: Place red peppers on greased grill over medium heat; cover and grill, turning often, until charred, 10 to 12 minutes. Place in bowl; cover and let cool. Peel, seed and thinly slice. Toss together peppers, oil, vinegar and salt; stir in basil.

In large saucepan, bring 4 cups water and salt to boil; reduce heat to low. Gradually whisk in cornmeal; cook, stirring often, for 10 minutes.

Add corn; cook until corn is tender-crisp and polenta is thick enough to mound on spoon, 5 to 10 minutes. Stir in cheese. Spread in greased 13- x 9-inch (3 L) baking dish. Let cool until set, about 30 minutes.

Cut polenta into 12 squares. Place on greased grill over medium heat; close lid and grill, turning once, until grill-marked, about 8 minutes. Serve topped with roasted red pepper mixture.

MAKES 6 SERVINGS. PER SERVING: about 180 cal, 6 g pro, 6 g total fat (2 g sat. fat), 28 g carb, 4 g fibre, 8 mg chol, 228 mg sodium, 200 mg potassium. % RDI: 10% calcium, 6% iron, 24% vit A, 166% vit C, 30% folate.

Leftovers from a holiday meal are inevitable, and pot pie is a delicious way to serve them. Apples add sweetness to this not-so-traditional version and complement the easy topping. You can shred the turkey instead of chopping it, if you prefer.

TURKEY POT PIE WITH CHEESE–CORN BREAD TOPPING

3 tbsp **butter**

1 **onion,** chopped

2 ribs **celery,** chopped

2 **sweet-tart apples** (such as Idared)

¼ cup **all-purpose flour**

3 cups **sodium-reduced chicken broth** or turkey stock

½ cup **milk**

3 cups chopped **cooked turkey**

3 **turkey sausages** (8 oz/225 g total), cooked and sliced

2 tbsp chopped **fresh parsley**

¼ tsp **pepper**

CHEESE–CORN BREAD TOPPING:

1 cup each **all-purpose flour** and **fine stone-ground cornmeal**

1 cup shredded **old Cheddar cheese**

2 **green onions,** thinly sliced

1 tbsp **granulated sugar**

2 tsp **baking powder**

1 cup **milk**

1 **egg**

3 tbsp **butter,** melted and cooled

¼ tsp **salt**

Pinch **pepper**

In Dutch oven, melt butter over medium heat; cook onion and celery, stirring occasionally, until celery begins to soften, 6 to 8 minutes.

Meanwhile, core and chop apples; add to pan. Cook until tender, about 5 minutes. Add flour; cook, stirring, for 1 minute. Stir in broth and milk; cook, stirring, for 5 minutes.

Stir in turkey, sausages, parsley and pepper; cook, stirring often, until sauce is thick enough to coat back of spoon, 10 to 12 minutes. Pour into 12-cup (3 L) casserole dish.

CHEESE–CORN BREAD TOPPING:

In bowl, whisk together flour, cornmeal, cheese, green onions, sugar and baking powder. Whisk together milk, egg, butter, salt and pepper; stir into cornmeal mixture. Spread evenly over casserole. Bake in 375°F (190°C) oven until light golden, 32 to 35 minutes.

MAKES 8 SERVINGS. PER SERVING: about 472 cal, 32 g pro, 20 g total fat (11 g sat. fat), 40 g carb, 3 g fibre, 125 mg chol, 741 mg sodium, 466 mg potassium. % RDI: 21% calcium, 20% iron, 17% vit A, 7% vit C, 37% folate.

Mushrooms add a huge amount of savoury flavour to any dish, and they are definitely one of the stars in this elegant vegetarian meal. Use a mixture of flavourful mushrooms, adjusting the mix to your taste and to what's freshest at the market. Cremini, shiitake, button or oyster mushrooms are usually easy to find.

POLENTA WITH MUSHROOM RAGOUT

2 tbsp **extra-virgin olive oil**

1⅔ lb (750 g) **mixed mushrooms,** quartered

1 **onion,** minced

2 cloves **garlic,** minced

1 tbsp minced **fresh thyme** (or 1 tsp dried thyme)

¼ tsp each **salt** and **pepper**

½ cup **dry white wine** or vegetable broth

1 tbsp **all-purpose flour**

1½ cups **vegetable broth**

¼ cup chopped **fresh parsley**

POLENTA:

3 cups **milk**

¼ tsp **salt**

1 cup **fine stone-ground cornmeal**

¼ cup grated **Parmesan cheese**

In Dutch oven, heat oil over medium-high heat; sauté mushrooms, onion, garlic, thyme, salt and pepper until no liquid remains, about 8 minutes.

Add wine; cook, stirring, until no liquid remains, about 4 minutes.

Add flour; stir to coat. Stir in broth and bring to boil; reduce heat and simmer, stirring occasionally, until slightly thickened, about 10 minutes. Stir in parsley.

POLENTA: Meanwhile, in large saucepan, bring milk, 1 cup water and salt to boil. Gradually whisk in cornmeal; simmer over medium-low heat, stirring, until thick enough to mound on spoon, about 15 minutes. Stir in Parmesan cheese. Serve topped with ragout.

MAKES 4 SERVINGS. PER SERVING: about 375 cal, 15 g pro, 13 g total fat (4 g sat. fat), 48 g carb, 6 g fibre, 20 mg chol, 843 mg sodium. % RDI: 29% calcium, 18% iron, 16% vit A, 12% vit C, 48% folate.

Clockwise from top left: Medium stone-ground cornmeal, popcorn and whole grain corn flour.

CORN

WHY IT'S GOOD FOR YOU: Sweet corn is eaten as a vegetable, while starchy field corn is dried, ground and used as a grain. Corn is gluten-free, so it's a delicious option for people with gluten intolerance. It contains lutein, which helps keep eyes healthy, and beta-carotene, a powerful antioxidant that turns into vitamin A in the body. Corn is also a source of magnesium and B vitamins (including niacin, folate and thiamine) and contains some fibre.

WHOLE GRAIN FORMS: Nutritious **stone-ground cornmeal** is made by grinding dried whole corn kernels (yellow, white or blue) using old-fashioned millstones. It comes in fine, medium and coarse grinds; all contain the nutrient-rich bran and germ. **Whole grain flour** can be made from corn, but check the label: Not all corn flour is created equal. Corn flour is not the same as cornstarch, which has no healthy whole grain properties. **Popcorn** kernels have moisture in the centre, which turns to steam when heated, exploding through the hull and popping out the tender interior of the kernel.

STORAGE: Whole grain cornmeal and flour contain natural oils that can go rancid. Refrigerate them in airtight containers for two months or freeze for up to six months. Unpopped popcorn is fine stored in an airtight jar in the pantry.

USES: Cornmeal adds crunch to breads, pancakes and baked goods. It's wonderful in polenta and porridge too. Popcorn is a high-fibre snack, but go easy on the toppings to keep it healthy.

For the best texture, make the jalapeño-infused corn bread a day ahead so it dries out a little. Serve with Classic Roast Turkey & Gravy (page 89).

JALAPEÑO CORN BREAD STUFFING WITH SMOKED SAUSAGE

1½ tsp **cumin seeds**

2 tbsp **vegetable oil**

8 oz (225 g) **kielbasa** or other smoked sausage, cubed

2 **onions,** chopped

2 ribs **celery,** chopped

4 cloves **garlic,** minced

1 tsp **dried oregano**

¼ tsp **pepper**

½ cup **turkey stock** or sodium-reduced chicken broth

JALAPEÑO CORN BREAD:

1¼ cups **fine stone-ground cornmeal**

¾ cup **all-purpose flour**

1 tbsp **granulated sugar**

1½ tsp **baking powder**

¾ tsp **baking soda**

½ tsp **salt**

1½ cups **buttermilk**

2 **eggs**

2 tbsp **butter,** melted

1 cup **cooked corn kernels**

2 tbsp minced **pickled jalapeño pepper**

JALAPEÑO CORN BREAD: In bowl, whisk together cornmeal, flour, sugar, baking powder, baking soda and salt. Whisk together buttermilk, eggs and butter; pour over dry ingredients. Sprinkle with corn and jalapeño pepper; stir just until combined. Scrape into parchment paper–lined or greased 8-inch (2 L) square cake pan; smooth top.

Bake in 375°F (190°C) oven until cake tester inserted in centre comes out clean, 30 minutes. Let cool in pan on rack for 5 minutes. Transfer to rack; let cool completely. *(Make-ahead: Wrap and refrigerate for up to 2 days.)*

In dry large skillet, toast cumin seeds over medium heat until fragrant, about 2 minutes. Transfer to large bowl.

In same skillet, heat half of the oil over medium-high heat; brown kielbasa. Add to cumin seeds.

Drain any fat from pan. Add remaining oil and heat over medium heat; fry onions, celery, garlic, oregano and pepper, stirring occasionally, until softened, about 8 minutes. Add to bowl. Coarsely crumble corn bread into bowl. Drizzle with turkey stock; mix well. *(Make-ahead: Cover and refrigerate for up to 24 hours.)*

Spoon stuffing into greased 9-inch (2.5 L) square cake pan. Cover with foil; bake in 400°F (200°C) oven for 20 minutes. Uncover; bake until crisp and golden, about 10 minutes.

MAKES 24 SERVINGS. PER SERVING: about 109 cal, 4 g pro, 5 g total fat (2 g sat. fat), 13 g carb, 1 g fibre, 26 mg chol, 229 mg sodium. % RDI: 4% calcium, 5% iron, 3% vit A, 3% vit C, 14% folate.

These delicate cakes may crumble a bit while being formed but will firm up during frying. Serve with a leafy green salad: two cakes for lighter appetites or three for hungrier folks.

QUINOA CAKES WITH LEMON YOGURT SAUCE

1½ cups **quinoa,** rinsed and drained

1½ cups **vegetable broth**

½ cup **olive oil**

Half **onion,** chopped

3 cloves **garlic,** minced

½ tsp **salt**

¼ tsp **pepper**

3 cups trimmed **fresh spinach**

3 **eggs**

¼ cup grated **Parmesan cheese**

2 tbsp **all-purpose flour**

1½ tsp **baking powder**

¼ tsp grated **lemon zest**

1 tbsp **sesame seeds,** pine nuts or sliced almonds, toasted

LEMON YOGURT SAUCE:

1½ cups **Balkan-style plain yogurt**

⅓ cup thinly sliced **green onions**

1 tbsp **lemon juice**

Pinch each **salt** and **pepper**

In saucepan, bring quinoa, broth and 1½ cups water to boil. Reduce heat, cover and simmer for 15 minutes. Drain in fine sieve; let cool completely in sieve.

Meanwhile, in skillet, heat 1 tbsp of the oil over medium heat; fry onion, garlic, salt and pepper, stirring occasionally, until onion is softened, about 4 minutes. Add spinach; cook, stirring, until wilted and no liquid remains, about 3 minutes. Let cool; coarsely chop.

LEMON YOGURT SAUCE: Stir together yogurt, green onions, lemon juice, salt and pepper. Set aside in refrigerator.

In large bowl, whisk together eggs, Parmesan cheese, flour, baking powder and lemon zest; fold in quinoa and spinach mixture. With wet hands, form into 16 cakes; transfer to waxed paper–lined tray. Refrigerate for 1 hour.

In nonstick skillet, heat half of the remaining oil over medium-high heat; fry half of the cakes, turning once with 2 spatulas, until golden, about 8 minutes. Keep warm on baking sheet in 200°F (100°C) oven. Repeat with remaining oil and cakes. Serve drizzled with yogurt sauce and sprinkled with sesame seeds.

MAKES ABOUT 8 SERVINGS. PER SERVING: about 353 cal, 11 g pro, 22 g total fat (5 g sat. fat), 30 g carb, 3 g fibre, 81 mg chol, 366 mg sodium, 454 mg potassium. % RDI: 17% calcium, 29% iron, 17% vit A, 7% vit C, 24% folate.

This is a vegetarian take on a traditional Greek and Turkish finger food. Look for grape leaves in Middle Eastern, Greek and Italian grocery stores. Most supermarkets carry them too, often in the pickle section.

QUINOA DOLMADES WITH TAHINI YOGURT SAUCE

36 **bottled grape leaves,** drained

1 tbsp **olive oil**

1 **onion,** diced

1 tsp **ground cumin**

½ tsp **ground coriander**

¼ tsp each **salt** and **pepper**

¼ tsp **cinnamon**

1 cup **quinoa,** rinsed and drained

⅓ cup **dried currants**

⅓ cup chopped **Kalamata olives**

⅓ cup **pine nuts,** toasted

¼ cup chopped **fresh mint**

1¼ cups **vegetable broth**

1 tbsp **lemon juice**

TAHINI YOGURT SAUCE:

1 cup **Balkan-style plain yogurt**

¼ cup **tahini**

2 tbsp chopped **fresh parsley**

2 tbsp warm **water**

1 tbsp **extra-virgin olive oil**

2 tsp **lemon juice**

¼ tsp each **salt** and **pepper**

TAHINI YOGURT SAUCE: Whisk together yogurt, tahini, parsley, water, oil, lemon juice, salt and pepper until smooth. Cover and set aside in refrigerator. *(Make-ahead: Refrigerate for up to 3 days.)*

In heatproof bowl, cover grape leaves with boiling water; let stand for 3 minutes. Drain well; let cool.

In saucepan, heat oil over medium heat; cook onion, stirring often, until softened, about 5 minutes. Stir in cumin, coriander, salt, pepper and cinnamon; cook for 1 minute. Add quinoa, currants and olives; cook, stirring, until quinoa is toasted, about 2 minutes.

Stir in 2 cups water; bring to boil. Reduce heat, cover and simmer until no liquid remains and quinoa is tender, 15 to 20 minutes. Let cool. Stir in pine nuts and mint.

Remove tough stems from grape leaves. Lay leaves, vein side up, on work surface. Place 1 tbsp filling in centre of each; fold in sides and roll snugly into cigar shapes.

Place dolmades, seam side down, in single layer in 13- x 9-inch (3 L) baking dish. Combine broth with lemon juice; pour over top.

Cover tightly with foil; bake in 350°F (180°C) oven until no liquid remains, about 1 hour. Let cool to room temperature. *(Make-ahead: Let cool for 30 minutes. Cover and refrigerate for up to 2 days.)*

Serve at room temperature or chilled with yogurt sauce for dipping.

MAKES 36 PIECES. PER PIECE: about 61 cal, 2 g pro, 4 g total fat (1 g sat. fat), 6 g carb, 1 g fibre, 1 mg chol, 205 mg sodium, 82 mg potassium. % RDI: 3% calcium, 6% iron, 1% vit A, 2% vit C, 4% folate.

This sweet and savoury stuffing is a perfect complement to a juicy pork roast. Serve with sautéed green beans for a special weekend dinner. Look for garam masala in the spice aisle at the supermarket, or try out different blends from an Indian grocery store.

ROASTED PORK LOIN WITH CURRIED APPLE QUINOA STUFFING

4 cloves **garlic,** minced

1 tbsp **garam masala**

1 tbsp **curry powder**

2 tsp packed **brown sugar**

2 tsp **dry mustard**

2 tsp **ground cumin**

1 tsp **salt**

½ tsp **pepper**

3 lb (1.35 kg) **boneless centre-cut pork loin roast**

1 tbsp **butter**

1 **onion,** chopped

1 **Granny Smith apple,** peeled and cut in ½-inch (1 cm) pieces

1¼ cups **sodium-reduced chicken broth**

¾ cup **quinoa,** rinsed and drained

⅓ cup **apple cider**

¼ cup finely chopped **fresh cilantro**

Mix together garlic, garam masala, curry powder, brown sugar, mustard, cumin, salt and pepper.

Butterfly pork roast (see Technique, opposite). Rub half of the spice mixture all over roast. Cover and refrigerate for 1 hour. *(Make-ahead: Refrigerate for up to 24 hours.)*

In large shallow saucepan, melt butter over medium-high heat. Add onion, apple and remaining spice mixture; cover and cook, stirring occasionally, until onion is softened, about 5 minutes.

Stir in broth, quinoa and cider; bring to boil. Reduce heat to low; cover and simmer until quinoa is almost tender, about 20 minutes. Remove from heat; let cool. Stir in cilantro.

Lay pork on work surface, fat side down and away from you. Leaving 1-inch (2.5 cm) border at edge farthest away from you, spread quinoa mixture evenly over pork; press lightly to compress. Starting at closest edge, roll up.

Evenly space eight 17-inch (43 cm) lengths of kitchen string on work surface; place pork, seam side up, across strings. Tie strings; cut off excess. Place pork, seam side down, in large roasting pan.

Roast in 400°F (200°C) oven, basting 3 times with pan juices, until juices run clear when pork is pierced and instant-read thermometer inserted in centre reads 160°F (71°C), about 1 hour.

Transfer to cutting board. Cover loosely with foil; let stand for 20 minutes before carving.

MAKES 8 TO 10 SERVINGS. PER EACH OF 10 SERVINGS: about 284 cal, 33 g pro, 10 g total fat (4 g sat. fat), 15 g carb, 2 g fibre, 71 mg chol, 378 mg sodium, 595 mg potassium. % RDI: 3% calcium, 20% iron, 2% vit A, 3% vit C, 6% folate.

TECHNIQUE:
BUTTERFLY A PORK ROAST

Sometimes a picture really is worth a thousand words. Here's how to butterfly a pork roast for Roasted Pork Loin With Curried Apple Quinoa Stuffing (opposite).

1 | Place pork, fat side up, on cutting board. Starting at long edge ½ inch (1 cm) from bottom of roast, cut 1-inch (2.5 cm) deep horizontal cut along length of roast.

2 | Continue making shallow horizontal cuts deeper into roast, from 1 end to the other, pushing away or "unrolling" meat as you cut. Keep your knife blade parallel to the cutting board to maintain the ½-inch (1 cm) thickness. (But don't worry if it isn't perfectly even.)

3 | Continue until you've cut through the entire loin to form a flat 12- x 10-inch (30 x 25 cm) rectangle.

Clockwise from top left: Whole grain amaranth flour, millet seeds and amaranth seeds

MILLET & AMARANTH

Millet is an ancient grain that's popular in African and some Asian cuisines. Amaranth is considered a whole grain food but is actually a seed; its leaves are eaten as a vegetable (similar to spinach), particularly in the Caribbean and China.

WHY THEY'RE GOOD FOR YOU: Both millet and amaranth are gluten-free and easily digestible, making them terrific options for people with celiac disease or gluten intolerance. Millet adds fibre to recipes and contains magnesium, B vitamins and zinc. Amaranth also offers up fibre, magnesium and zinc, and adds a dose of manganese to the mix.

WHOLE GRAIN FORMS: Millet and amaranth **seeds** are the whole, unprocessed kernels of the plants. They're similar looking, but amaranth seeds are tinier and look a bit like mustard seeds. **Whole grain flour** can be made from both amaranth and millet. The flours are gluten-free, so they'll need help from other flours or ingredients to make breads and baked goods rise.

STORAGE: Both grains are high in natural fats and can spoil quickly. Keep them in airtight containers in the freezer for up to six months.

USES: Mix millet and amaranth with other grains to make whole grain porridge for breakfast. Millet makes excellent stuffings, and it's wonderful in stuffed vegetables. Try out millet and amaranth flours in gluten-free baking recipes, or add millet to traditional breads for an extra crunch.

Available in the health food section of grocery stores and in natural food stores, mildly flavoured millet is a perfect backdrop to all kinds of seasonings. Here, it's an interesting alternative to regular rice stuffing.

MILLET & SAUSAGE-STUFFED PEPPERS

1⅓ cups **vegetable broth**

⅔ cup **millet**

3 **mild Italian sausages,** casings removed

1 tbsp **vegetable oil**

⅓ cup **pine nuts**

1 small **onion,** diced

2 cloves **garlic,** minced

¼ cup drained **oil-packed sun-dried tomatoes,** chopped

¼ tsp each **salt** and **pepper**

Pinch **cinnamon**

¼ cup chopped **fresh basil** or fresh parsley

4 **sweet red peppers** or sweet yellow peppers

In saucepan, bring broth to boil; stir in millet. Reduce heat, cover and simmer until no liquid remains, about 25 minutes.

Meanwhile, in skillet, sauté sausage over medium-high heat, breaking up with spoon, until browned, about 8 minutes. Transfer to paper towel–lined plate. Drain fat from pan.

Add oil to pan; toast pine nuts over medium heat, stirring, until light golden, about 2 minutes. Stir in onion, garlic, tomatoes, salt, pepper and cinnamon; fry, stirring, until onions are softened, about 5 minutes.

In bowl, combine cooked millet, sausage, onion mixture and basil.

Cut peppers in half lengthwise; with spoon, remove seeds and ribs. Fill pepper halves with millet mixture; place in roasting pan just large enough to hold peppers snugly.

Pour ⅔ cup water into pan; cover with lightly greased foil. Bake in 400°F (200°C) oven until peppers are tender, about 55 minutes.

MAKES 4 SERVINGS. PER SERVING: about 436 cal, 18 g pro, 24 g total fat (5 g sat. fat), 40 g carb, 6 g fibre, 32 mg chol, 824 mg sodium. % RDI: 4% calcium, 21% iron, 47% vit A, 342% vit C, 22% folate.

Middle Eastern tabbouleh is usually made with bulgur, a whole grain form of wheat. By using quinoa, which is an excellent source of iron, this salad becomes gluten-free.

QUINOA TABBOULEH

¾ cup **quinoa,** rinsed and drained

1 cup chopped **fresh flat-leaf parsley**

1 cup chopped **English cucumber**

½ cup chopped **green onions**

¼ cup chopped **fresh mint**

1 **tomato,** seeded and chopped

DRESSING:

3 tbsp **lemon juice**

2 tbsp **extra-virgin olive oil**

¼ tsp each **salt** and **pepper**

In saucepan, bring 1½ cups water to boil; add quinoa and return to boil. Reduce heat, cover and simmer until no liquid remains, about 18 minutes. Remove from heat; fluff with fork. Transfer to bowl; let cool.

Add parsley, cucumber, green onions, mint and tomato.

DRESSING: Whisk together lemon juice, oil, salt and pepper; pour over quinoa mixture and toss to coat. Serve at room temperature or cover and refrigerate for 1 hour.

TIP: Quinoa has a natural coating of saponin, a white powdery substance that tastes bitter and soapy. Before using quinoa, soak it in water for 5 minutes, then rinse well under cold running water to remove any traces of this coating.

MAKES 6 SERVINGS. PER SERVING: about 135 cal, 4 g pro, 6 g total fat (1 g sat. fat), 18 g carb, 3 g fibre, 0 mg chol, 112 mg sodium, 335 mg potassium. % RDI: 4% calcium, 24% iron, 13% vit A, 33% vit C, 18% folate.

The amount of water you need to cook different kinds of quinoa varies, so check package directions for best results. For a crunchy twist, top this salad with toasted slivered almonds.

GLUTEN-FREE QUINOA SALAD WITH CREAMY TAHINI DRESSING

1 cup **quinoa,** rinsed and drained

½ tsp **salt**

¼ cup **lemon juice**

¼ cup **extra-virgin olive oil**

¼ cup **tahini**

¼ cup warm **water**

1 small clove **garlic,** minced

½ tsp **ground cumin**

¼ tsp **pepper**

2 cups **grape tomatoes** or cherry tomatoes, halved

1 cup diced **English cucumber**

1 cup drained rinsed **canned lentils**

⅔ cup chopped **fresh parsley**

⅓ cup chopped **fresh mint**

3 **green onions,** thinly sliced

In saucepan, bring quinoa, half of the salt and 2 cups water to boil over high heat; reduce heat, cover and simmer until no liquid remains and quinoa is tender, about 15 minutes. Let cool.

In large bowl, whisk together lemon juice, oil, tahini, warm water, garlic, cumin, pepper and remaining salt.

Stir in quinoa, tomatoes, cucumber, lentils, parsley, mint and green onions; toss to coat. (Make-ahead: Cover and refrigerate for up to 3 days.)

MAKES 4 TO 6 SERVINGS. PER EACH OF 6 SERVINGS: about 300 cal, 9 g pro, 16 g total fat (2 g sat. fat), 32 g carb, 6 g fibre, 0 mg chol, 291 mg sodium, 581 mg potassium. % RDI: 9% calcium, 43% iron, 12% vit A, 33% vit C, 48% folate.

The combination of barley and quinoa gives this dish a healthy mix of soluble and insoluble fibre. The ginger vinaigrette is delightfully tangy and is delicious on a green salad as well.

WHOLE GRAIN QUINOA & BARLEY SALAD

¼ tsp **salt**

⅔ cup **pot barley**

⅔ cup **quinoa,** rinsed and drained

1 tbsp **extra-virgin olive oil**

½ cup each finely diced **carrot, celery** and **onion**

½ cup each finely diced **sweet red pepper** and **zucchini**

½ cup finely diced **cucumber**

1 tbsp chopped **fresh parsley**

1 tbsp chopped **fresh mint**

1 tsp chopped **fresh thyme**

GINGER VINAIGRETTE:

¼ cup **extra-virgin olive oil**

2 tbsp **white wine vinegar**

1 tsp grated **fresh ginger** (or ¼ tsp ground ginger)

1 tsp **Dijon mustard**

¼ tsp each **salt** and **pepper**

In saucepan, bring 1⅔ cups water and half of the salt to boil; add barley. Reduce heat to low; cover and simmer gently until tender and liquid is absorbed, about 50 minutes. Let cool.

Meanwhile, in separate saucepan, bring 1 cup water and remaining salt to boil; add quinoa. Reduce heat, cover and simmer until tender and liquid is absorbed, about 15 minutes. Let cool.

Meanwhile, in skillet, heat oil over medium heat; cook carrot, celery, onion, red pepper and zucchini, stirring occasionally, until tender-crisp, about 5 minutes. Let cool.

GINGER VINAIGRETTE: Whisk together oil, vinegar, ginger, mustard, salt and pepper.

In large bowl, combine barley, quinoa, vegetable mixture, cucumber, parsley, mint and thyme; pour vinaigrette over top. Toss to coat. (*Make-ahead: Cover and refrigerate for up to 24 hours.*)

MAKES 6 SERVINGS. PER SERVING: about 264 cal, 6 g pro, 13 g total fat (2 g sat. fat), 33 g carb, 6 g fibre, 0 mg chol, 229 mg sodium, 389 mg potassium. % RDI: 4% calcium, 21% iron, 23% vit A, 42% vit C, 13% folate.

Clockwise from top left: White quinoa seeds, whole grain quinoa flour and red quinoa seeds

QUINOA

WHY IT'S GOOD FOR YOU: This nutritious ancient grain is technically a seed, but it is considered a whole grain. Native to South America, quinoa was a staple for the Incan civilization. It is a complete protein and a source of iron, zinc, manganese, magnesium and folate. It also contains fibre. Quinoa is gluten-free, so it's a great choice for people with celiac disease and gluten intolerance.

WHOLE GRAIN FORMS: Quinoa **seeds** are natural and unprocessed. Quinoa is a trendy staple in North American cuisine, so it's easy to find in supermarkets, health food stores and bulk food stores. **Whole grain flour** made from quinoa is often available in health food stores and bulk food stores. It's a protein-packed, gluten-free option for baking.

STORAGE: Keep uncooked quinoa fresh by refrigerating it in an airtight container for up to six months. You can refrigerate cooked quinoa for up to three days. Store quinoa flour in the freezer.

USES: Quinoa is coated with saponin, a bitter substance that protects the seeds. Many brands wash off this coating, but to be sure, before cooking, soak quinoa in warm water for 5 minutes, then rinse well under cold water to remove any traces of bitterness. Cooked quinoa shines in salads, stuffings and side dishes – and even mixed-grain porridge. Try it in place of bread crumbs as a coating on baked or fried chicken or fish. Yellow and red varieties are equally nutritious, but red is prettier in salads and cooks up a bit firmer.

This tasty summer salad is wonderful with fresh beans from the farmer's market or the garden. Serve it alongside your favourite grilled meat or fish, or serve larger portions as a vegetarian main.

QUINOA & CHICKPEA SALAD WITH TOMATO VINAIGRETTE

1 cup **quinoa,** rinsed and drained

2 cups **green beans,** trimmed and chopped

1 can (19 oz/540 mL) **chickpeas,** drained and rinsed

1 **sweet red pepper,** diced

1 cup crumbled **feta cheese**

TOMATO VINAIGRETTE:

⅓ cup **bottled strained tomatoes** (passata)

3 tbsp **red wine vinegar**

3 tbsp **olive oil**

3 tbsp **liquid honey**

½ tsp each **dried Italian herb seasoning** and **salt**

¼ tsp **pepper**

Pinch **cayenne pepper**

In saucepan, bring quinoa and 2 cups water to boil; reduce heat, cover and simmer for 12 minutes. Fluff with fork; let cool.

Meanwhile, in saucepan of boiling salted water, blanch green beans until tender-crisp, about 3 minutes. Drain and chill in bowl of ice water. Drain and transfer to large bowl.

Stir in quinoa, chickpeas, red pepper and feta cheese.

TOMATO VINAIGRETTE: Whisk together strained tomatoes, vinegar, oil, honey, Italian seasoning, salt, pepper and cayenne pepper; pour over quinoa mixture. Stir to coat.

MAKES 4 SERVINGS. PER SERVING: about 556 cal, 18 g pro, 22 g total fat (8 g sat. fat), 75 g carb, 9 g fibre, 35 mg chol, 1,155 mg sodium, 649 mg potassium. % RDI: 25% calcium, 46% iron, 18% vit A, 108% vit C, 53% folate.

This moist, sweet and spicy corn bread is the perfect side dish for your next backyard barbecue. If you love heat, add another jalapeño pepper. To omit the ale, just substitute the same amount of buttermilk.

JALAPEÑO GREEN ONION ALE CORN BREAD

1 cup **fine stone-ground cornmeal**

1 cup **all-purpose flour**

1 tsp **baking powder**

½ tsp each **baking soda** and **salt**

½ cup **granulated sugar**

½ cup **buttermilk**

½ cup **brown ale** or Pilsner beer

½ cup **butter,** melted

2 **eggs**

1 **jalapeño pepper,** seeded and diced

4 **green onions,** chopped

In large bowl, whisk together cornmeal, flour, baking powder, baking soda and salt. Whisk together sugar, buttermilk, ale, butter and eggs; whisk into flour mixture. Fold in jalapeño pepper and green onions; scrape into parchment paper–lined 8- x 4-inch (1.5 L) loaf pan.

Bake in 375°F (190°C) oven until golden and cake tester inserted in centre comes out clean, about 40 minutes.

Let cool in pan on rack for 2 minutes. Transfer to rack; let cool slightly. Serve warm or at room temperature.

MAKES 1 LOAF, OR 10 TO 12 SLICES. PER EACH OF 12 SLICES: about 192 cal, 4 g pro, 9 g total fat (5 g sat. fat), 24 g carb, 1 g fibre, 52 mg chol, 248 mg sodium, 81 mg potassium. % RDI: 3% calcium, 6% iron, 9% vit A, 2% vit C, 20% folate.

Spoonbread is a soft, spoonable version of corn bread that's wonderful seasoned with cheese and aromatic garlic and onions. It's easy to make and is a delicious alternative to stuffing.

CHEDDAR & LEEK SPOONBREAD

2 tbsp **butter**

3 cloves **garlic,** minced

3 **leeks** (white and light green parts only), thinly sliced

2 cups **milk**

1½ cups **sodium-reduced chicken broth** or vegetable broth

½ tsp **cayenne pepper**

½ tsp **salt**

1½ cups **fine stone-ground cornmeal**

4 **eggs,** separated

1½ cups shredded **old Cheddar cheese**

In large saucepan, melt butter over medium-high heat; sauté garlic and leeks until softened, 6 to 7 minutes.

Stir in milk, broth, cayenne pepper and ¼ tsp of the salt; bring to simmer. Whisking constantly, pour in cornmeal in slow steady stream; cook until bubbly, 1 to 2 minutes. Remove from heat. Briskly whisk in egg yolks. Set aside.

In bowl, beat egg whites with remaining salt until soft peaks form, 2 to 3 minutes. Stir one-quarter into cornmeal mixture to loosen; fold in remaining whites. Fold in 1 cup of the Cheddar cheese. Scrape into greased 8-inch (2 L) square baking dish or round casserole dish; sprinkle with remaining cheese. Bake in 350°F (180°C) oven until golden, 30 to 35 minutes.

MAKES 8 TO 10 SERVINGS. PER EACH OF 10 SERVINGS: about 232 cal, 11 g pro, 11 g total fat (6 g sat. fat), 22 g carb, 2 g fibre, 102 mg chol, 374 mg sodium, 185 mg potassium. % RDI: 19% calcium, 7% iron, 13% vit A, 3% vit C, 23% folate.

Cornmeal and multigrain flour combine to make a pleasing, perfectly crunchy corn bread. No multigrain flour? Use ⅓ cup each all-purpose flour and whole wheat flour.

CHEDDAR & SAGE SKILLET CORN BREAD

1¾ cups **medium stone-ground cornmeal**

⅔ cup **multigrain flour**

1 tbsp **granulated sugar**

2 tsp **baking powder**

½ tsp **salt**

2 **eggs**

1½ cups **milk**

1 cup shredded **old Cheddar cheese**

1 tbsp chopped **fresh sage** (or 1 tsp dried sage)

2 tbsp **butter**

In large bowl, whisk cornmeal, flour, sugar, baking powder and salt. In separate bowl, beat eggs until foamy; whisk in milk. Pour over cornmeal mixture; sprinkle with half of the cheese and the sage. Stir just until combined.

In ovenproof 10-inch (25 cm) cast-iron skillet, melt butter in 450°F (230°C) oven until smoking, about 6 minutes. Scrape batter into hot skillet; sprinkle with remaining cheese.

Bake until golden and firm to the touch, 25 minutes. Let cool in pan on rack for 5 minutes. Invert onto rack; invert top side up. Let cool. *(Make-ahead: Store in airtight container for up to 2 days or wrap in plastic wrap and freeze in airtight container for up to 2 weeks.)*

MAKES 8 TO 12 SERVINGS. PER EACH OF 12 SERVINGS: about 188 cal, 7 g pro, 7 g total fat (4 g sat. fat), 24 g carb, 2 g fibre, 48 mg chol, 242 mg sodium. % RDI: 12% calcium, 6% iron, 8% vit A, 20% folate.

The mixture of grains gives this handsome loaf a sweet but earthy flavour. Serve slices with stews, such as Green Chili Pork Stew (opposite), or enjoy them with coffee or tea as a snack.

CORNMEAL & WHOLE WHEAT QUICK BREAD

1¼ cups **all-purpose flour**

½ cup **whole wheat flour**

½ cup **fine stone-ground cornmeal**

⅓ cup **natural bran**

¼ cup packed **brown sugar**

1½ tsp **baking soda**

½ tsp **salt**

⅔ cup **buttermilk**

⅔ cup **butter,** melted

3 tbsp **liquid honey**

2 **eggs**

Stir together all-purpose flour, whole wheat flour, all but 2 tbsp of the cornmeal, the bran, brown sugar, baking soda and salt.

In large bowl, stir together buttermilk, butter, honey and eggs; stir in flour mixture. Scrape into parchment paper–lined 8- x 4-inch (1.5 L) loaf pan; sprinkle with remaining cornmeal.

Bake in 350°F (180°C) oven until cake tester inserted in centre comes out clean, about 50 minutes. Let cool in pan on rack for 10 minutes. Transfer to rack; let cool.

MAKES 1 LOAF, OR ABOUT 12 SLICES. PER SLICE: about 232 cal, 5 g pro, 12 g total fat (7 g sat. fat), 29 g carb, 2 g fibre, 59 mg chol, 350 mg sodium, 119 mg potassium. % RDI: 3% calcium, 9% iron, 10% vit A, 20% folate.

This southwest-inspired stew is a wonderful complement to any of our tasty corn breads. It's made directly in the slow cooker without any browning beforehand, so it's the ideal set-and-forget meal.

GREEN CHILI PORK STEW

2 lb (900 g) **boneless pork shoulder,** cubed

1 **white onion,** diced

4 cloves **garlic,** minced

2 tsp each **ground cumin** and **dried oregano**

½ tsp **salt**

1 can (19 oz/540 mL) **pinto beans** or romano beans, drained and rinsed

1 cup **mild salsa**

2 cans (127 mL each) **chopped green chilies,** drained and rinsed

½ cup **sodium-reduced chicken broth**

3 tbsp **all-purpose flour**

¼ cup chopped **fresh cilantro**

In slow cooker, combine pork, onion, garlic, cumin, oregano and salt. Stir in beans, salsa, green chilies and broth.

Cover and cook on high until pork is tender, 6 to 8 hours.

Whisk flour with 3 tbsp water until smooth; whisk into slow cooker. Cook, covered, on high until slightly thickened, about 20 minutes. Stir in cilantro.

MAKES 6 SERVINGS. PER SERVING: about 404 cal, 35 g pro, 19 g total fat (7 g sat. fat), 25 g carb, 6 g fibre, 101 mg chol, 922 mg sodium, 880 mg potassium. % RDI: 8% calcium, 31% iron, 3% vit A, 28% vit C, 38% folate.

These savoury treats are sure to be a hit with people who love corn bread. Medium-ground cornmeal gives these muffins a slightly crunchy texture, while frozen corn keeps them moist, even though the recipe only calls for 2 tbsp butter. Serve them warm with a bowl of chili or corn chowder.

LIGHTENED-UP MINI CORN MUFFINS

1 cup **medium stone-ground cornmeal**

¼ cup **all-purpose flour**

2 tbsp **granulated sugar**

½ tsp **baking soda**

¼ tsp **salt**

Pinch **cayenne pepper**

1 cup **buttermilk**

1 **egg**

2 tbsp **butter,** melted

⅔ cup **frozen corn kernels**

In large bowl, whisk together cornmeal, flour, sugar, baking soda, salt and cayenne pepper.

Whisk together buttermilk, egg and butter; pour over cornmeal mixture. Sprinkle with corn; stir just until combined. Spoon into greased mini–muffin cups.

Bake in 400°F (200°C) oven until cake tester inserted in a few comes out clean, about 10 minutes. Let cool in pan on rack. *(Make-ahead: Store in airtight container for up to 2 days or freeze for up to 2 weeks.)*

MAKES 24 MINI-MUFFINS. PER MINI-MUFFIN: about 48 cal, 1 g pro, 2 g total fat (1 g sat. fat), 7 g carb, 1 g fibre, 11 mg chol, 69 mg sodium, 49 mg potassium. % RDI: 2% calcium, 1% iron, 2% vit A, 3% folate.

These scones have a light, fluffy texture with a hint of sweetness and the pleasant crunch of millet. Ancient grains and flours, such as kamut, millet and quinoa, are increasingly easy to find in stores.

ANCIENT GRAINS SCONES

1¾ cups **all-purpose flour**

1 cup **kamut flour**

½ cup **millet**

2½ tsp **baking powder**

½ tsp each **baking soda** and **salt**

½ cup cold **butter,** cubed

1 cup **buttermilk**

¼ cup **liquid honey**

1 **egg**

In large bowl, whisk together all-purpose and kamut flours, millet, baking powder, baking soda and salt. Using pastry blender or 2 knives, cut in butter until in coarse crumbs. Whisk together buttermilk, honey and egg; with fork, stir into flour mixture to make soft dough.

With floured hands, press dough into ball. On floured surface, knead dough 10 times. Pat out into 10- x 7-inch (25 x 18 cm) rectangle; trim sides to straighten.

Cut rectangle into 6 squares; cut each diagonally in half. Place on large parchment paper–lined rimmed baking sheet.

Bake in 400°F (200°C) oven until golden, 18 to 20 minutes. Transfer to rack; let cool. *(Make-ahead: Store in airtight container for up to 24 hours or wrap individually in plastic wrap and freeze in airtight container for up to 2 weeks.)*

MAKES 12 SCONES. PER SCONE: about 207 cal, 5 g pro, 9 g total fat (5 g sat. fat), 28 g carb, 3 g fibre, 37 mg chol, 290 mg sodium. % RDI: 6% calcium, 9% iron, 8% vit A, 4% folate.

Whole wheat flour and blueberries put a spin on the classic crispy cornmeal muffin. Light-tasting olive oil may seem like an unusual addition, but it's flavour-neutral and a source of healthy monounsaturated fat.

CORNMEAL BLUEBERRY MUFFINS

½ cup **granulated sugar**

1 tsp grated **lemon zest**

1 cup **fine stone-ground cornmeal**

⅔ cup **all-purpose flour**

⅓ cup **whole wheat flour**

4 tsp **baking powder**

¼ tsp **salt**

1 cup fresh or frozen **wild blueberries**

1 cup **milk**

1 **egg**

⅓ cup **light-tasting olive oil** or safflower oil

In bowl, rub sugar with lemon zest; whisk in cornmeal, all-purpose and whole wheat flours, baking powder and salt. Toss blueberries with 1 tbsp of the flour mixture.

In large bowl, whisk together milk, egg and oil; stir in flour mixture just until combined. Stir in blueberries. Spoon into 12 paper-lined or greased muffin cups.

Bake in 400°F (200°C) oven until tops are firm to the touch, about 20 minutes.

Let cool in pan on rack for 2 minutes. Transfer to rack; let cool. *(Make-ahead: Store in airtight container for up to 2 days.)*

MAKES 12 MUFFINS. PER MUFFIN: about 189 cal, 3 g pro, 7 g total fat (1 g sat. fat), 28 g carb, 2 g fibre, 17 mg chol, 163 mg sodium, 88 mg potassium. % RDI: 7% calcium, 6% iron, 2% vit A, 2% vit C, 15% folate.

From left: Cornmeal Blueberry Muffins
(page 197), Fig & Pecan Muffins (page 47) and
Banana, Date & Oat Bran Muffins (page 248)

These rustic cornmeal S-shaped cookies are a delicious change of pace from traditional sweet cookies. The cornmeal gives them a pleasant crunch that goes well with a cup of tea. Dust them with icing sugar, if desired.

LEMON CORNMEAL COOKIES

1⅓ cups **all-purpose flour**

1⅓ cups **fine stone-ground cornmeal**

1 cup cold **butter,** cubed

3 **egg yolks**

1 cup packed **brown sugar**

1 tsp **vanilla**

1 tsp grated **lemon zest**

In large bowl, whisk flour with cornmeal; using pastry blender or 2 knives, cut in butter until crumbly.

Beat together egg yolks, brown sugar and vanilla until thickened, about 5 minutes. Scrape over flour mixture. Add lemon zest; beat at medium speed just until blended. (Dough will be stiff.)

On work surface and working with ¼ cup batter at a time, roll and shape into 15-inch (38 cm) long ropes. Cut into 3-inch (8 cm) lengths; bend into S shapes. Place, 1 inch (2.5 cm) apart, on parchment paper–lined rimless baking sheets. Refrigerate for 30 minutes.

Bake in top and bottom thirds of 375°F (190°C) oven, rotating and switching pans halfway through, until golden, 10 to 12 minutes.

Let cool on pans on racks for 3 minutes. Transfer cookies to racks; let cool. *(Make-ahead: Layer between waxed paper in airtight container and store for up to 4 days or freeze for up to 1 month.)*

MAKES ABOUT 84 COOKIES. PER COOKIE: about 65 cal, 1 g pro, 3 g total fat (2 g sat. fat), 8 g carb, trace fibre, 20 mg chol, 33 mg sodium. % RDI: 1% calcium, 2% iron, 3% vit A, 3% folate.

Serve this ultrapopular Indian spiced tea hot or iced with Gluten-Free Amaranth Spice Cookies (opposite). Dried orange zest and ginger give a burst of fresh flavour to the homemade Chai Tea Mix (below).

CHAI TEA FOR TWO

1 cup **milk**

1 cup **water**

2 tbsp **Chai Tea Mix** (right)

Granulated sugar (optional)

In saucepan, bring milk and water to boil; remove from heat. Stir in chai tea mix; cover and steep for 5 minutes.

Strain into warmed mugs. Stir in sugar (if using) to taste.

TIP: To make with tea bags, mix together the spices for Chai Tea Mix (right), omitting tea. Prepare milk and water as directed. Steep 2 tea bags and 1 tbsp of the spice mixture. Let stand for 5 minutes. Sweeten as desired.

MAKE YOUR OWN
Chai Tea Mix

Peel 1 piece (1 inch/2.5 cm) fresh ginger; cut into ⅛-inch (3 mm) thick slices. Arrange on rack. Using vegetable peeler, peel zest from 1 large orange (avoiding white pith); add to rack. Let dry at room temperature until brittle, about 24 hours.

In bowl, break zest and 4 sticks (each 3 inches/8 cm long) cinnamon into 1-inch (2.5 cm) pieces. Add ginger; 1 cup black tea leaves (such as Darjeeling); 24 green cardamom pods, crushed; and 12 whole cloves. Mix well. (*Make-ahead: Store in airtight container for up to 2 months.*)

MAKES 2 CUPS.

MAKES 2 SERVINGS. PER SERVING: about 63 cal, 4 g pro, 2 g total fat (2 g sat. fat), 7 g carb, 0 g fibre, 9 mg chol, 68 mg sodium. % RDI: 13% calcium, 1% iron, 6% vit A, 2% vit C, 8% folate.

Amaranth has a sweet, almost grassy flavour that works well with the spices in this recipe. These gluten-free cookies bake up deliciously crisp on the edges and soft and chewy in the middle – the best of both worlds.

GLUTEN-FREE AMARANTH SPICE COOKIES

¾ cup **butter,** softened

1 cup packed **dark brown sugar**

¼ cup **fancy molasses**

1 **egg**

1½ cups **gluten-free all-purpose baking flour**

¾ cup **amaranth flour**

1 tsp **cinnamon**

½ tsp **ground ginger**

½ tsp **ground cloves**

¼ tsp **nutmeg**

½ tsp **salt**

In large bowl, beat butter with brown sugar until fluffy. Beat in molasses, scraping down side of bowl. Beat in egg until smooth.

Whisk together gluten-free flour, amaranth flour, cinnamon, ginger, cloves, nutmeg and salt. Stir into butter mixture just until combined.

Drop by rounded 1 tbsp, about 2 inches (5 cm) apart, onto parchment paper–lined rimless baking sheets. Bake, 1 pan at a time, in 350°F (180°C) oven until edges are golden, 12 to 14 minutes.

Let cool on pan on rack for 2 minutes. Transfer to rack; let cool.

TIP: All-purpose gluten-free baking flour is a blend of starches and gluten-free flours that can take the place of all-purpose wheat flour in some baked goods. Brands such as Bob's Red Mill are available in health food stores and many supermarkets.

MAKES 35 TO 40 COOKIES. PER EACH OF 40 COOKIES: about 83 cal, 1 g pro, 4 g total fat (2 g sat. fat), 12 g carb, 1 g fibre, 14 mg chol, 58 mg sodium, 62 mg potassium. % RDI: 2% calcium, 4% iron, 3% vit A, 1% folate.

This rustic loaf is hearty and flavourful, with a mix of different grains, including cornmeal and crunchy millet. It makes the most delicious toast.

CRUNCHY CRISSCROSS BREAD

½ tsp **granulated sugar**

1 cup warm **water**

2 tsp **active dry yeast**

2 tbsp **liquid honey**

2 tbsp **butter,** melted

1 **egg**

2½ cups **all-purpose flour** (approx)

¾ cup **whole wheat flour**

¼ cup **quick-cooking rolled oats**

¼ cup **fine stone-ground cornmeal**

¼ cup **natural bran**

¼ cup **millet** or sesame seeds

1 tsp **salt**

In large bowl, dissolve sugar in warm water. Sprinkle in yeast; let stand until frothy, about 10 minutes.

Whisk in honey, butter and egg. Stir in 2 cups of the all-purpose flour, whole wheat flour, oats, cornmeal, bran, millet and salt until smooth. Gradually stir in enough of the remaining all-purpose flour to form slightly sticky dough.

Turn out onto lightly floured surface; knead, dusting with as much of the remaining flour as needed to prevent sticking, until smooth and elastic, 8 to 10 minutes. Place in greased bowl, turning to grease all over. Cover with plastic wrap; let rise in warm draft-free place until doubled in bulk, about 1½ hours.

Punch down dough; turn out onto floured surface. Shape into rounded loaf, pulling dough down all around and pinching underneath to smooth top. Dust top with flour; place on greased rimless baking sheet. Cover and let rise in warm draft-free place until doubled in bulk, 45 to 60 minutes.

Using serrated knife, slash shallow grid pattern on top of loaf. Bake in 375°F (190°C) oven until golden and loaf sounds hollow when tapped on bottom, 45 minutes. Transfer to rack; let cool.

CHANGE IT UP

Crisscross Flax Bread

Omit bran. Replace cornmeal with ¼ cup ground flaxseeds; replace millet with ¼ cup whole flaxseeds. Increase second rise time to 60 to 75 minutes. Bake as directed.

MAKES 1 LOAF, OR 24 SLICES. PER SLICE: about 113 cal, 3 g pro, 2 g total fat (1 g sat. fat), 21 g carb, 2 g fibre, 12 mg chol, 109 mg sodium. % RDI: 1% calcium, 8% iron, 1% vit A, 10% folate.

This soft, creamy corn bread is delicious drizzled with extra maple syrup or served with ice cream for dessert. For an indulgent brunch, make it the night before and keep it in the fridge overnight. Cut slices ½ inch (1 cm) thick and fry in skillet over high heat, turning once, until browned on both sides; dust with icing sugar.

MAPLE PECAN SPOONBREAD

1⅔ cups **milk**

⅓ cup **whipping cream** (35%)

⅓ cup **maple syrup**

¼ cup **granulated sugar**

1 tsp **vanilla**

½ tsp **salt**

½ tsp **maple extract**

1½ cups **fine stone-ground cornmeal**

4 **eggs,** separated

1 cup **canned 100% pumpkin** (not pie filling)

TOPPING:
¼ cup **butter**

¼ cup **maple syrup**

1 cup chopped **pecans**

In saucepan, stir together milk, 1 cup water, cream, maple syrup, sugar, vanilla, salt and maple extract. Bring to simmer over medium heat; whisking constantly, add cornmeal in steady stream. Cook until bubbly, 1 to 2 minutes. Remove from heat. Briskly whisk in egg yolks; stir in pumpkin.

In large bowl, beat egg whites until soft peaks form. Stir one-quarter into cornmeal mixture until loose; fold in remaining whites. Scrape into greased 8-inch (2 L) square baking dish or round casserole dish; smooth top.

TOPPING: In small skillet over medium-high heat, melt butter with maple syrup; bring to simmer. Stir in pecans; spread evenly over cornmeal mixture.

Bake in 350°F (180°C) oven until edges are golden and centre is no longer jiggly, about 45 minutes. Let cool for 10 minutes before serving.

MAKES 8 TO 10 SERVINGS. PER EACH OF 10 SERVINGS: about 334 cal, 7 g pro, 19 g total fat (7 g sat. fat), 37 g carb, 4 g fibre, 100 mg chol, 196 mg sodium, 285 mg potassium. % RDI: 8% calcium, 11% iron, 40% vit A, 2% vit C, 8% folate.

Coated in a mixture of chili powder and sugar, this perfect sweet-and-salty snack is a great way to start a get-together. It also makes a great grab-bag treat to send home with guests – especially for kids' birthday parties.

SWEET CHILI POPCORN

12 cups warm freshly popped **popcorn**
¼ cup **unsalted butter**
¼ cup packed **brown sugar**
2 tsp **chili powder**
¼ tsp **salt**

Place popcorn in extra-large bowl; set aside.

In small saucepan, bring butter, sugar, chili powder and salt to simmer over medium heat, stirring constantly; cook, stirring, until smooth, about 2 minutes.

Immediately pour chili mixture over popcorn; toss to coat.

TIP: Air-popped popcorn is light and fluffy, without added oil. It's perfect for this type of treat. It also makes a nutritious whole grain snack when you're not in the mood for a salty-sweet indulgence like this.

MAKES 12 CUPS. PER ½ CUP: about 42 cal, 1 g pro, 2 g total fat (1 g sat. fat), 6 g carb, 1 g fibre, 5 mg chol, 27 mg sodium, 25 mg potassium. % RDI: 1% iron, 2% vit A.

From left: Caramel
Almond Popcorn
(opposite) and
Sweet Chili Popcorn
(page 207)

This old-time favourite is an ideal treat for adults and children alike. You'll need one bag of microwave popcorn or ½ cup unpopped kernels to make the amount of popped corn called for.

CARAMEL ALMOND POPCORN

10 cups warm freshly popped **popcorn**

2 cups **natural almonds**

1¼ cups packed **brown sugar**

½ cup **unsalted butter**

¼ cup **light corn syrup**

2 tsp **vanilla**

¼ tsp **baking soda**

Grease large rimmed baking sheet; mix warm popcorn with almonds on baking sheet. Set aside.

In saucepan, whisk together brown sugar, butter and corn syrup over medium-low heat until sugar is dissolved. Increase heat to high; boil, without stirring, until candy thermometer registers hard-ball stage of 255°F (124°C), or ½ tsp syrup dropped into very cold water forms rigid ball that is still a little pliable, about 4 minutes.

Remove pan from heat. Stir in vanilla and baking soda.

Drizzle over popcorn mixture, stirring gently until combined. Let cool completely. *(Make-ahead: Store in airtight container for up to 1 week.)*

MAKES 12 CUPS. PER 1 CUP: about 337 cal, 6 g pro, 20 g total fat (6 g sat. fat), 37 g carb, 3 g fibre, 21 mg chol, 43 mg sodium. % RDI: 8% calcium, 11% iron, 7% vit A, 7% folate.

BARLEY & OATS

Serve this perfect weekend breakfast with milk and maple syrup, or top with a spoonful of Cinnamon Fruit Compote (page 223). Instead of almonds, you can use dried cranberries, dried blueberries or raisins.

MAPLE-BAKED OATMEAL

1½ cups **large-flake rolled oats**

¼ cup **sliced almonds**

2 tbsp packed **maple sugar** or brown sugar

2 tbsp **maple syrup**

Pinch **salt**

3 cups **milk**

Cinnamon

In greased 8-inch (2 L) square baking dish, combine oats, almonds, maple sugar, maple syrup and salt; stir in milk.

Bake in 350°F (180°C) oven until oats are softened and milk is absorbed, about 40 minutes.

Sprinkle with cinnamon to taste. Serve hot.

MAKES 4 SERVINGS. PER SERVING: about 309 cal, 13 g pro, 9 g total fat (3 g sat. fat), 46 g carb, 4 g fibre, 14 mg chol, 97 mg sodium. % RDI: 24% calcium, 16% iron, 9% vit A, 2% vit C, 10% folate.

Dried papaya, pineapple and mango infuse toothsome oats with tropical flavours. This makes a great sunny-tasting breakfast for a cold, blustery morning.

STEEL-CUT OATS WITH TROPICAL FRUITS

2 cups **milk**

1 cup **steel-cut oats**

¼ cup each chopped **dried papaya, dried pineapple** and **dried mango**

2 **whole cloves**

¼ tsp each **ground allspice** and **salt**

Pinch **nutmeg**

In saucepan, bring milk and 2½ cups water to boil. Stir in oats, papaya, pineapple, mango, cloves, allspice, salt and nutmeg; return to boil.

Reduce heat; simmer, uncovered and stirring often, until oats are tender, 35 minutes. Discard cloves.

MAKES 4 SERVINGS. PER SERVING: about 227 cal, 8 g pro, 4 g total fat (2 g sat. fat), 42 g carb, 4 g fibre, 10 mg chol, 202 mg sodium. % RDI: 17% calcium, 9% iron, 13% vit A, 37% vit C, 4% folate.

Top to bottom:
Oat groats, large-flake rolled
oats and steel-cut oats

PROFILE:
OATS

WHY THEY'RE GOOD FOR YOU: Oats, whether they're rolled or steel-cut, are a good source of soluble and insoluble fibre. One type of fibre found in this versatile grain, called beta-glucan, is known for its cholesterol-lowering effects and has been linked to blood sugar stabilization, which may make it a good carbohydrate choice for people with type 2 diabetes. Pure uncontaminated oats (processed in wheat-free facilities) are considered gluten-free.

WHOLE GRAIN FORMS: Oat **groats** are the whole berries (or kernels) of the oat plant. **Steel-cut oats** are groats that have been cut into roughly thirds; sometimes they're known as pinhead oats, Scottish oats or Irish oats. **Rolled oats** are – you guessed it – rolled to flatten them so that they cook more quickly. Rolled oats come in a variety of thicknesses: Large-flake (a.k.a. old-fashioned) are the thickest, quick-cooking are thinner, and instant rolled oats are thinner still and cut into very small pieces so that they're ready to eat when stirred with boiling water. **Whole grain flour** made from oats is good for baking, but is often mixed with gluten-containing flours because it can give baked goods an overly dense texture when used alone.

STORAGE: Oats aren't as perishable as many other whole grains, so they'll keep in an airtight container in the pantry for several months.

USES: Oats are good for more than just porridge and muesli. They're ideal for crumble toppings, as a meatloaf filler (instead of bread crumbs), and in muffins, breads, snack bars, cookies and granola.

Golden fruits and crunchy nuts dot this tasty breakfast granola with their bright and earthy flavours. It's like sunshine in a bowl. Try it sprinkled over ice cream or yogurt for a simple dessert.

GOLDEN GRANOLA

5 cups **large-flake rolled oats**

½ cup **raw cashew halves**

½ cup **natural almonds,** chopped

½ cup sliced **dried apricots**

½ cup **banana chips**

⅓ cup chopped **dried mango**

⅓ cup **sweetened shredded coconut**

¼ cup **unsalted raw hulled sunflower seeds**

⅓ cup **liquid honey**

¼ cup **brown rice syrup**

¼ cup **canola oil** or coconut oil, melted

¼ tsp **salt**

½ cup **golden raisins**

In large bowl, toss together oats, cashews, almonds, apricots, banana chips, mango, coconut and sunflower seeds.

In small saucepan over medium heat, warm together honey, brown rice syrup, oil and salt, stirring, until blended, about 3 minutes. Pour over oat mixture; toss to coat.

Spread evenly on 2 greased or parchment paper–lined rimmed baking sheets. Bake in 325°F (160°C) oven for 15 minutes.

Stir in raisins; rotate pans and bake, stirring once, until granola is golden and fragrant, about 15 minutes. Let cool on pans on racks. *(Make-ahead: Store in airtight container for up to 3 weeks.)*

MAKES 9 CUPS. PER ¼ CUP: about 132 cal, 3 g pro, 5 g total fat (1 g sat. fat), 19 g carb, 2 g fibre, 0 mg chol, 23 mg sodium, 127 mg potassium. % RDI: 1% calcium, 7% iron, 1% vit A, 2% vit C, 3% folate.

This sweet granola is so addictive that you'll want it for snacking anytime, not just for breakfast. The recipe is good for people who have to avoid gluten but can still tolerate oats. Look for "wheat-free" or "gluten-free" labelling on the oats to ensure there is no cross-contamination.

CRUNCHY GLUTEN-FREE GRANOLA

5 cups **wheat-free rolled oats** (such as Bob's Red Mill Gluten-Free Rolled Oats)

½ cup chopped **hazelnuts**

½ cup chopped **almonds**

⅓ cup **unsalted raw hulled sunflower seeds**

⅓ cup **unsalted raw hulled pumpkin seeds**

⅓ cup **dried cranberries**

⅓ cup sliced **dried apricots**

¼ cup **raisins**

¼ cup packed **brown sugar**

2 tbsp **flaxseeds**

2 tbsp **sesame seeds**

⅓ cup **brown rice syrup**

¼ cup **liquid honey**

¼ cup **canola oil** (or butter, melted)

½ tsp **cinnamon**

½ tsp **salt**

In large bowl, combine oats, hazelnuts, almonds, sunflower seeds, pumpkin seeds, cranberries, apricots, raisins, brown sugar, flaxseeds and sesame seeds.

In saucepan over medium heat, warm together brown rice syrup, honey, oil, cinnamon and salt, stirring, until blended, about 3 minutes. Pour over oat mixture; toss to coat.

Spread evenly on 2 greased or parchment paper–lined rimmed baking sheets. Bake in 325°F (160°C) oven, stirring every 10 minutes and rotating pans halfway through, until golden, about 25 minutes.

Let cool on pans on racks. (*Make-ahead: Store in airtight container for up to 3 weeks.*)

MAKES 9 CUPS. PER ¼ CUP: about 133 cal, 4 g pro, 6 g total fat (1 g sat. fat), 18 g carb, 2 g fibre, 0 mg chol, 37 mg sodium, 124 mg potassium. % RDI: 2% calcium, 9% iron, 1% vit A, 5% folate.

From left: Crunchy Gluten-Free
Granola (page 217), Autumn
Harvest Granola (page 221),
Chocolate Cherry Granola (page
220) and Golden Granola (page 216)

You won't miss the nuts in this deluxe granola. Make sure it is completely cool before adding the chocolate.

CHOCOLATE CHERRY GRANOLA

1 pkg (453 g) **five-grain rolled cereal** (such as Bob's Red Mill Five-Grain Rolled Cereal) or large-flake rolled oats (about 4½ cups)

¾ cup **unsalted raw hulled pumpkin seeds**

½ cup **dried sour cherries**

½ cup **dried cranberries**

½ cup chopped **dates**

⅓ cup **unsalted raw hulled sunflower seeds**

2 tbsp **sesame seeds**

½ cup **unsweetened applesauce**

⅓ cup **maple syrup**

¼ cup **canola oil** (or butter, melted)

½ tsp **vanilla**

¼ tsp **salt**

½ cup chopped **bittersweet chocolate** (or semisweet chocolate chips)

In large bowl, toss together cereal, pumpkin seeds, sour cherries, cranberries, dates, sunflower seeds and sesame seeds.

In small saucepan over medium heat, warm together applesauce, maple syrup, oil, vanilla and salt, stirring, until thinned, about 3 minutes. Pour over cereal mixture; toss to coat.

Spread evenly on 2 greased or parchment paper–lined rimmed baking sheets. Bake in 325°F (160°C) oven, stirring every 5 minutes and rotating pans halfway through, until golden, about 30 minutes.

Let cool completely on pans on racks. Stir in chocolate. *(Make-ahead: Store in airtight container for up to 3 weeks.)*

MAKES 8 CUPS. PER ¼ CUP: about 140 cal, 4 g pro, 6 g total fat (1 g sat. fat), 20 g carb, 3 g fibre, 0 mg chol, 20 mg sodium, 90 mg potassium. % RDI: 2% calcium, 9% iron, 1% vit A, 3% folate.

Don't let the long ingredient list fool you. Homemade granola takes only a few minutes to pull together before popping it into the oven. Use lightly greased kitchen shears to quickly and easily cut up dried fruit.

AUTUMN HARVEST GRANOLA

4 cups **large-flake rolled oats**

½ cup **pecan halves,** coarsely chopped

½ cup **slivered almonds**

½ cup chopped **dried apples**

½ cup chopped **dried pears**

⅓ cup chopped **hazelnuts**

⅓ cup **dried cranberries**

⅓ cup **raisins**

¼ cup **unsalted raw hulled pumpkin seeds**

2 tbsp **flaxseeds**

2 tbsp packed **brown sugar**

½ cup **unsweetened applesauce**

⅓ cup **liquid honey**

¼ cup **canola oil** (or butter, melted)

¼ tsp **salt**

¼ tsp each **ground ginger** and **cinnamon**

In large bowl, combine oats, pecans, almonds, apples, pears, hazelnuts, cranberries, raisins, pumpkin seeds, flaxseeds and brown sugar.

In saucepan over medium heat, warm together applesauce, honey, oil, salt, ginger and cinnamon, stirring, until thinned, about 3 minutes. Pour over oat mixture; toss to coat.

Spread evenly on 2 greased or parchment paper–lined rimmed baking sheets. Bake in 325°F (160°C) oven, stirring every 10 minutes and rotating pans halfway through, until golden, 30 to 35 minutes.

Let cool on pans on racks. *(Make-ahead: Store in airtight container for up to 3 weeks.)*

MAKES 8 CUPS. PER ¼ CUP: about 141 cal, 3 g pro, 6 g total fat (1 g sat. fat), 20 g carb, 3 g fibre, 0 mg chol, 23 mg sodium, 141 mg potassium. % RDI: 2% calcium, 8% iron, 2% vit C, 3% folate.

Rolled oats are a good source of soluble fibre, which helps keep blood sugar steady and makes you feel full longer. This is a wonderful balanced breakfast for mornings when you're on the go.

SWISS MUESLI WITH FRESH FRUIT

1 cup **large-flake rolled oats**

1 cup **fat-free fruit-flavoured yogurt**

1 cup **skim milk**

½ cup **sliced almonds**

¼ cup **dried cranberries**

¼ cup **dried blueberries** or dried currants

1 **Granny Smith apple,** cored and diced

2 cups **fresh fruit** (such as sliced strawberries, sliced nectarines, sliced pears, raspberries and/or blueberries)

In airtight container, stir together oats, yogurt, milk, almonds, cranberries, blueberries and apple.

Seal and refrigerate for 8 hours. *(Make-ahead: Refrigerate for up to 3 days.)*

Serve with fruit.

MAKES 4 SERVINGS. PER SERVING: about 312 cal, 12 g pro, 9 g total fat (1 g sat. fat), 51 g carb, 8 g fibre, 2 mg chol, 40 mg sodium. % RDI: 14% calcium, 14% iron, 7% vit A, 37% vit C, 12% folate.

Spooning this compote over hot or cold cereal means that no extra sugar is needed. It's also luscious spooned over Oatmeal Buttermilk Pancakes (page 224) or Best-Ever Whole Grain Pancakes (page 17).

CINNAMON FRUIT COMPOTE

1 cup chopped **dried apricots**

½ cup chopped **dried apples**

½ cup **dried cranberries**

½ cup chopped **dates**

⅓ cup packed **brown sugar**

2 strips (1 inch/2.5 cm wide each) **lemon zest**

2 tbsp **lemon juice**

1 **cinnamon stick** (or 1½ tsp ground cinnamon)

In saucepan, bring apricots, apples, cranberries, dates, brown sugar, lemon zest, lemon juice, cinnamon stick and 2 cups water to boil. Reduce heat to medium-low; cover and simmer until fruit is tender, about 20 minutes.

Discard lemon zest and cinnamon stick. Let cool. *(Make-ahead: Refrigerate in airtight container for up to 1 week.)*

*TIP: This recipe is great for large groups and school breakfast programs. Just double the recipe and use 2 saucepans to make 24 servings.

MAKES 3 CUPS, OR 12 SERVINGS. PER SERVING: about 95 cal, 1 g pro, trace total fat (0 g sat. fat), 25 g carb, 2 g fibre, 0 mg chol, 7 mg sodium. % RDI: 1% calcium, 6% iron, 8% vit A, 3% vit C.

Oats and whole wheat flour add fibre and nutty flavour to these pancakes. They're delicious with good old-fashioned maple syrup and butter, or a dollop of Cinnamon Fruit Compote (page 223).

OATMEAL BUTTERMILK PANCAKES

2¼ cups **buttermilk**

1½ cups **quick-cooking rolled oats** (not instant)

½ cup **all-purpose flour**

½ cup **whole wheat flour**

1 tbsp packed **brown sugar**

1 tsp **baking powder**

1 tsp **baking soda**

¼ tsp **salt**

2 **eggs**

3 tbsp **vegetable oil**

Combine buttermilk with oats; let stand for 5 minutes.

In bowl, whisk together all-purpose and whole wheat flours, brown sugar, baking powder, baking soda and salt. Whisk eggs with 2 tbsp of the oil; pour over dry ingredients. Scrape buttermilk mixture over top; stir just until combined.

Lightly brush large nonstick skillet with some of the remaining oil; heat over medium heat. Using about ¼ cup for each pancake, pour in batter. Cook until underside is golden and bubbles break on top that do not fill in, 1½ to 2 minutes.

Turn pancakes; cook until underside is golden, 30 to 60 seconds.

Repeat with remaining batter, brushing skillet with some of the remaining oil as needed between batches. (*Make-ahead: Let cool. Stack pancakes, separated by waxed paper, and freeze in resealable freezer bag for up to 2 weeks. Reheat in toaster.*)

MAKES ABOUT 15 PANCAKES. PER PANCAKE: about 123 cal, 5 g pro, 5 g total fat (1 g sat. fat), 15 g carb, 1 g fibre, 28 mg chol, 184 mg sodium. % RDI: 6% calcium, 6% iron, 2% vit A, 8% folate.

These crunchy home-baked Scottish-style crackers are the perfect base for rich, flavourful Whisky Cheddar Spread (opposite) or your favourite cheese.

OATCAKES

2 cups **large-flake rolled oats**

½ cup **walnut pieces**

1 cup **all-purpose flour**

2 tbsp packed **brown sugar**

1 tsp **baking powder**

½ tsp **salt**

½ cup cold **butter,** cubed

¾ cup **buttermilk**

In food processor, pulse oats with walnuts until powdery with some small pieces remaining; transfer to bowl. Whisk in flour, brown sugar, baking powder and salt.

Using pastry blender or 2 knives, cut in butter until crumbly; stir in buttermilk to form stiff smooth dough. Press into disc; wrap and refrigerate for 30 minutes. *(Make-ahead: Refrigerate for up to 24 hours.)*

On lightly floured surface, roll out dough to scant ¼-inch (5 mm) thickness. With 2-inch (5 cm) round cookie cutter, cut out circles, rerolling scraps. Place, 1 inch (2.5 cm) apart, on parchment paper–lined or greased rimless baking sheets.

Bake in top and bottom thirds of 350°F (180°C) oven, switching and rotating pans halfway through, until edges are crisp and golden, about 28 minutes.

Let cool on pans on racks for 5 minutes. Transfer to racks; let cool completely. *(Make-ahead: Store in airtight container for up to 2 days or freeze for up to 1 month.)*

MAKES ABOUT 40 PIECES. PER PIECE: about 64 cal, 1 g pro, 4 g total fat (2 g sat. fat), 7 g carb, 1 g fibre, 7 mg chol, 64 mg sodium. % RDI: 1% calcium, 3% iron, 2% vit A, 3% folate.

A creamy, irresistible spread like this is an excellent make-in-advance dish to serve at a party. It's particularly nice paired with homemade Oatcakes (opposite).

WHISKY CHEDDAR SPREAD

⅓ cup **hazelnuts**

2 cups diced **extra-old Cheddar cheese** (10 oz/280 g), at room temperature

¼ cup **butter,** softened

2 tbsp **Scotch whisky**

1 tbsp **Dijon mustard**

½ tsp **pepper**

On small rimmed baking sheet, toast hazelnuts in 350°F (180°C) oven until golden and fragrant, about 6 minutes. Let cool; coarsely chop.

In food processor, purée together Cheddar cheese, butter, whisky, mustard and pepper until smooth. Pulse in ¼ cup of the hazelnuts just until mixed.

Scrape into bowl; sprinkle with remaining hazelnuts. *(Make-ahead: Cover and refrigerate for up to 3 days.)*

CHANGE IT UP
Creamy Cheddar Spread
Substitute milk for the whisky.

MAKES 2 CUPS. PER 1 TBSP: about 57 cal, 3 g pro, 5 g total fat (3 g sat. fat), trace carb, trace fibre, 14 mg chol, 76 mg sodium. % RDI: 6% calcium, 1% iron, 4% vit A, 1% folate.

A smoked turkey leg or drumstick creates a rich base for this hearty root vegetable and barley soup. Leftovers make a great lunch the following day, or can be frozen for later.

CHUNKY VEGETABLE BARLEY SOUP

2 tbsp **vegetable oil**

1 **onion,** diced

2 each **carrots** and ribs **celery,** diced

1 lb (450 g) **mini red potatoes,** scrubbed and diced

12 oz (340 g) **white turnips,** diced

2 **parsnips,** diced

1 tsp **dried thyme**

½ tsp **salt**

¼ tsp **pepper**

¾ cup **pot barley** or pearl barley

¼ cup chopped **fresh parsley**

SMOKED TURKEY STOCK:

1 lb (450 g) **smoked turkey leg** or smoked drumstick

1 each **onion, carrot** and rib **celery,** quartered

8 oz (225 g) **mushrooms,** halved

8 **black peppercorns**

3 sprigs **fresh parsley**

1 **bay leaf**

SMOKED TURKEY STOCK: Remove skin and meat from turkey, reserving bone and discarding skin. Cut meat into bite-size pieces; set aside. In Dutch oven, combine turkey bone, onion, carrot, celery, mushrooms, peppercorns, parsley, bay leaf and 12 cups water; bring to boil. Reduce heat, cover and simmer until flavourful, about 4 hours. Strain stock to make about 8 cups. Set aside. *(Make-ahead: Let cool for 30 minutes; refrigerate in airtight container for up to 3 days.)*

In clean Dutch oven, heat oil over medium heat; cook onion, carrots and celery, stirring occasionally, until softened, about 5 minutes.

Add potatoes, turnips, parsnips, thyme, salt and pepper; cook, stirring occasionally, for 5 minutes. Add barley; cook, stirring, for 1 minute.

Add smoked turkey stock and 2 cups water; bring to boil. Reduce heat, cover and simmer until barley is tender, about 40 minutes.

Stir in reserved turkey meat and parsley; cook for 5 minutes. *(Make-ahead: Let cool for 30 minutes; refrigerate in airtight container for up to 3 days.)*

MAKES 12 TO 16 SERVINGS. PER EACH OF 16 SERVINGS: about 157 cal, 10 g pro, 5 g total fat (1 g sat. fat), 19 g carb, 3 g fibre, 18 mg chol, 318 mg sodium, 455 mg potassium. % RDI: 4% calcium, 12% iron, 17% vit A, 18% vit C, 14% folate.

You can make this robust soup as spicy as you like by adjusting the kind of curry paste you use: mild, medium or hot. A dollop of yogurt in each bowl is an attractive garnish and cools the fire of hot curry spices.

SLOW-COOKER CURRIED MUSHROOM BARLEY LENTIL SOUP

1 tbsp **vegetable oil**

1 large **onion,** chopped

4 cloves **garlic,** minced

6 cups sliced **mushrooms** (1 lb/450 g)

1 tbsp minced **fresh ginger**

1 tbsp **curry paste**

¼ tsp each **salt** and **pepper**

6 cups **vegetable broth,** Roasted Vegetable Stock (opposite) or beef broth

½ cup **dried green lentils**

⅓ cup **pot barley** or pearl barley

In skillet, heat oil over medium heat; fry onion, garlic, mushrooms, ginger, curry paste, salt and pepper, stirring often, until no liquid remains, about 10 minutes. Scrape into slow cooker.

Add broth, lentils and barley to slow cooker. Cover and cook on low until vegetables are tender, 6 to 8 hours.

MAKES 8 TO 10 SERVINGS. PER EACH OF 10 SERVINGS: about 102 cal, 4 g pro, 3 g total fat (trace sat. fat), 16 g carb, 3 g fibre, 0 mg chol, 480 mg sodium. % RDI: 2% calcium, 13% iron, 5% vit C, 28% folate.

Richly flavoured and coloured, this stock is wonderful in soups, such as Slow-Cooker Curried Mushroom Barley Lentil Soup (opposite). For even deeper flavour, add a couple of dried shiitake mushrooms when the stock is simmering.

ROASTED VEGETABLE STOCK

3 **carrots,** coarsely chopped

3 **onions,** coarsely chopped

3 ribs **celery,** coarsely chopped

1 cup sliced **mushrooms** (stems and/or caps)

3 cloves **garlic**

2 tsp **vegetable oil**

10 sprigs **fresh parsley**

10 **black peppercorns,** cracked

2 **bay leaves**

8 cups cold **water**

½ tsp **salt**

In large roasting pan, stir carrots, onions, celery, mushrooms, garlic and oil to coat. Roast in 450°F (230°C) oven, stirring halfway through, until softened and browned, about 40 minutes. Transfer to stockpot.

Add parsley, peppercorns, bay leaves and all but 1 cup of the water to pot. Pour remaining water into roasting pan, stirring and scraping up browned bits from bottom of pan, over heat if necessary. Scrape into pot; bring to boil. Skim off any foam. Reduce heat to medium; simmer until flavourful, about 1 hour.

Strain through fine sieve, gently pressing vegetables. Stir in salt. *(Make-ahead: Let cool for 30 minutes; refrigerate in airtight container for up to 3 days or freeze for up to 4 months.)*

MAKES ABOUT 5 CUPS. PER ½ CUP: about 33 cal, 1 g pro, 1 g total fat (0 g sat. fat), 5 g carb, 0 g fibre, 0 mg chol, 145 mg sodium. % RDI: 2% calcium, 4% iron, 57% vit A, 13% vit C, 8% folate.

Barley can soak up a lot of liquid. If this hearty soup ends up too thick, adjust the consistency by adding more broth or water. Serve with slices of whole grain bread to soak up the tasty broth.

BEEF & POT BARLEY SOUP

2 tbsp **vegetable oil**

1 lb (450 g) **stewing beef cubes**

2 tbsp **all-purpose flour**

2 **onions,** chopped

3 cloves **garlic,** minced

3 cups sliced **mushrooms**
  (8 oz/225 g)

2 each **carrots** and ribs **celery,**
  chopped

1 tsp **dried thyme**

½ tsp crumbled **dried sage**

5 cups **beef broth**

½ cup **red wine**

1 can (19 oz/540 mL) **whole
  tomatoes**

½ tsp **pepper**

¼ tsp **salt**

½ cup **pot barley**

In large heavy saucepan or Dutch oven, heat oil over medium-high heat. Toss beef with flour; in batches, brown all over, about 5 minutes. Transfer to plate. Drain any fat from pan.

Increase heat to high; cook onions, garlic, mushrooms, carrots, celery, thyme and sage, stirring, until no liquid remains, 5 minutes. Stir in broth and wine; cook for 1 minute, stirring and scraping up any browned bits from bottom of pan.

Return beef to pan along with 2 cups water, tomatoes, pepper and salt; bring to boil. Cover, reduce heat and simmer for 30 minutes.

Add barley; simmer until beef and barley are tender, 1 hour. *(Make-ahead: Let cool for 30 minutes; refrigerate, uncovered, in shallow airtight container until cold. Cover and refrigerate for up to 2 days.)*

MAKES 6 TO 8 SERVINGS. PER EACH OF 8 SERVINGS: about 233 cal, 16 g pro, 10 g total fat (3 g sat. fat), 21 g carb, 4 g fibre, 34 mg chol, 1,036 mg sodium, 564 mg potassium. % RDI: 5% calcium, 24% iron, 36% vit A, 22% vit C, 11% folate.

Cabbage rolls often contain a mix of meat and grains, but these barley-stuffed ones are a delicious whole grain vegetarian version. Start them in a slow cooker on a weekend morning, then head out for a busy day of errands or fun. Their delicious smell will welcome you home to a leisurely dinner.

BARLEY TOMATO CABBAGE ROLLS

1 head **cabbage** (3½ lb/1.58 kg)

1 tbsp **vegetable oil**

1 **onion,** chopped

1 clove **garlic,** minced

1 tsp **dried oregano**

½ tsp **dried thyme**

½ tsp each **salt** and **pepper**

¼ tsp **caraway seeds** (optional), crushed

1 cup **pot barley**

2 cups **vegetable broth**

1 each **carrot** and **zucchini,** diced

1 **egg,** beaten

2½ cups **tomato juice**

¼ cup **tomato paste**

1 tsp **granulated sugar**

1 can (28 oz/796 mL) **sauerkraut,** rinsed and squeezed dry

Core cabbage. In large pot of boiling salted water, cover and heat cabbage until leaves are softened and easy to remove, about 8 minutes. Chill in cold water. Without tearing, carefully remove 12 leaves, returning cabbage to pot for 2 to 3 minutes if leaves become difficult to remove. Drain on towels. Pare off coarse veins; set leaves aside.

In saucepan, heat oil over medium heat; fry onion, garlic, oregano, thyme, salt, pepper, and caraway seeds (if using), stirring often, until softened, about 5 minutes.

Stir in barley. Add broth; bring to boil. Reduce heat, cover and simmer until barley is tender and liquid is absorbed, about 40 minutes. Stir in carrot and zucchini. Let cool. Stir in egg.

Spoon rounded ⅓ cup barley mixture onto each cabbage leaf just above stem. Fold bottom and sides over filling; roll up.

Whisk together tomato juice, tomato paste and sugar. Spread one-third of the sauerkraut in slow cooker. Arrange half of the cabbage rolls on top, seam side down. Arrange half of the remaining sauerkraut over rolls; pour half of the tomato mixture over top. Top with remaining cabbage rolls, sauerkraut, then tomato mixture.

Place foil directly on surface. Cover and cook on low until cabbage is tender, about 7 hours.

MAKES 6 SERVINGS. PER SERVING: about 251 cal, 7 g pro, 5 g total fat (1 g sat. fat), 49 g carb, 10 g fibre, 31 mg chol, 1,817 mg sodium. % RDI: 10% calcium, 32% iron, 42% vit A, 90% vit C, 42% folate.

Nutritious whole grain barley is a delicious substitute for refined short-grain rice in risottos. Here, it partners with woodsy mushrooms and freshly shaved Parmesan cheese to make a creamy main dish.

MUSHROOM BARLEY RISOTTO

1 cup **boiling water**

1 pkg (14 g) **mixed dried mushrooms**

3 cups **sodium-reduced chicken broth**

2 tbsp **olive oil**

1 small **onion,** diced

3 **green onions,** sliced

1 clove **garlic,** minced

1 cup sliced **cremini mushrooms**

1¼ cups **pot barley**

1 tbsp chopped **fresh flat-leaf parsley**

Pinch **salt**

¼ cup shaved **Parmesan cheese**

In heatproof bowl, pour boiling water over dried mushrooms; let stand for 30 minutes. Reserving soaking liquid, drain; coarsely chop mushrooms. Set aside.

In saucepan, bring reserved soaking liquid, broth and 2½ cups water to simmer; reduce heat and keep warm.

In separate saucepan, heat oil over medium-high heat; cook onion, green onions and garlic until fragrant and softened, about 3 minutes.

Add soaked mushrooms and cremini mushrooms; sauté until almost no liquid remains, about 5 minutes.

Add barley; cook, stirring to coat, for 1 minute. Reduce heat to medium. Add hot broth mixture, ½ cup at a time and stirring after each addition until liquid is absorbed before adding more, until creamy and barley is tender but still slightly firm, about 45 minutes total.

Stir in parsley and salt. Serve topped with Parmesan cheese.

MAKES 6 SERVINGS. PER SERVING: about 224 cal, 9 g pro, 7 g total fat (2 g sat. fat), 33 g carb, 8 g fibre, 4 mg chol, 406 mg sodium, 290 mg potassium. % RDI: 10% calcium, 12% iron, 9% vit A, 3% vit C, 7% folate.

At first, it may look like there's too much dressing for this delicious sweet and savoury salad, but the barley and apricots will absorb most of it. Brighten up the flavour by stirring ¼ cup chopped fresh parsley into the salad just before serving.

SUMMERTIME WHOLE GRAIN BARLEY SALAD

1¾ cups **pot barley**

1 clove **garlic,** minced

¼ cup **cider vinegar**

2 tbsp **lemon juice**

4 tsp **Dijon mustard**

¾ tsp **salt**

¼ tsp **pepper**

¼ cup **extra-virgin olive oil**

1 cup diced **medium Gouda cheese** or aged Gouda cheese

½ cup diced **dried apricots**

⅓ cup **salted roasted hulled pumpkin seeds**

In large pot of boiling lightly salted water, cook barley until tender, about 30 minutes. Drain and rinse under cold water; drain again.

In large bowl, combine garlic, vinegar, lemon juice, mustard, salt and pepper; gradually whisk in oil until combined.

Add barley, Gouda cheese and apricots; stir to combine. Cover and refrigerate for 4 hours. *(Make-ahead: Refrigerate for up to 24 hours.)*

To serve, toss with pumpkin seeds.

MAKES 6 TO 8 SERVINGS. PER EACH OF 8 SERVINGS: about 339 cal, 13 g pro, 17 g total fat (5 g sat. fat), 37 g carb, 8 g fibre, 19 mg chol, 848 mg sodium, 388 mg potassium. % RDI: 13% calcium, 19% iron, 14% vit A, 2% vit C, 7% folate.

With its nutty, chewy texture, this healthful salad makes a satisfying lunch. It's enough for two lunch servings, which is great if you don't want to be eating the same salad for a week, but you can easily double it to make more.

WHOLE GRAIN BARLEY MUSHROOM SALAD

⅓ cup **pot barley**

¼ cup chopped **green beans**

2 tbsp chopped **walnuts**

2 tsp **butter**

2 tsp **extra-virgin olive oil**

1 cup sliced **mushrooms**

Half rib **celery,** diced

LEMON DRESSING:

1 tbsp minced **fresh parsley**

1 tbsp **extra-virgin olive oil**

1 tbsp **lemon juice**

1 clove **garlic,** minced

1 small **shallot** or green onion, minced

1 tsp **Dijon mustard**

Pinch each **salt** and **pepper**

In saucepan of boiling salted water, cover and cook barley until tender, about 30 minutes. Add green beans; cook until tender-crisp, 3 minutes. Drain and chill under cold water; drain and return to pot.

In dry skillet, toast walnuts over medium-low heat until fragrant, 2 minutes; add to barley mixture.

In same skillet, melt butter with oil over medium-high heat; sauté mushrooms until light golden, about 4 minutes. Add to barley mixture along with celery.

LEMON DRESSING: In jar, shake together parsley, oil, lemon juice, garlic, shallot, mustard, salt and pepper; toss with barley mixture. *(Make-ahead: Refrigerate in airtight container for up to 24 hours.)*

MAKES 2 SERVINGS. PER SERVING: about 312 cal, 7 g pro, 21 g total fat (5 g sat. fat), 28 g carb, 7 g fibre, 10 mg chol, 419 mg sodium, 367 mg potassium. % RDI: 4% calcium, 14% iron, 13% vit A, 12% vit C, 13% folate.

If you can't find oat groats for this fresh salad, substitute wheat berries, whole spelt berries, brown rice or any whole grain, cooking according to package directions.

HONEY-LIME OAT & BLACK BEAN SALAD

1 cup **oat groats**

1 cup rinsed drained **canned black beans**

1 cup halved **cherry tomatoes**

1 **jalapeño pepper,** seeded and finely chopped

2 tbsp finely chopped **red onion**

Half ripe **avocado,** diced

1 tbsp chopped **fresh cilantro**

HONEY-LIME VINAIGRETTE:
3 tbsp **vegetable oil**

1 tsp grated **lime zest**

3 tbsp **lime juice**

1 tbsp **liquid honey**

¼ tsp **chili powder**

¼ tsp each **salt** and **pepper**

In large saucepan, bring 2 cups water to boil; add oats. Reduce heat and simmer, uncovered and stirring occasionally, until tender and no water remains, about 45 minutes. Drain and rinse under cold water; drain again.

HONEY-LIME VINAIGRETTE:
Meanwhile, whisk together oil, lime zest, lime juice, honey, chili powder, salt and pepper.

In large bowl, combine oats, black beans, tomatoes, jalapeño pepper and onion. Add vinaigrette and toss to coat. Cover and refrigerate for 1 hour. *(Make-ahead: Refrigerate for up to 24 hours.)*

To serve, stir in avocado; sprinkle with cilantro.

MAKES 6 SERVINGS. PER SERVING: about 241 cal, 7 g pro, 11 g total fat (1 g sat. fat), 30 g carb, 6 g fibre, 0 mg chol, 205 mg sodium, 368 mg potassium. % RDI: 3% calcium, 14% iron, 3% vit A, 17% vit C, 17% folate.

Pot barley adds a pleasant whole grain chewiness to this hearty salad. If your feta cheese tastes especially salty, soak it for 30 minutes in cold water and drain before crumbling it.

MEDITERRANEAN RICE & POT BARLEY SALAD

1 cup **pot barley**

1 cup **basmati rice**

3 cups **cherry tomatoes,** halved

Half large **red onion,** cut in 1-inch (2.5 cm) chunks

1 **sweet red pepper,** cut in 1-inch (2.5 cm) chunks

1 **English cucumber** cut in 1-inch (2.5 cm) chunks

4 cups **fresh baby spinach,** coarsely chopped

1 pkg (200 g) **feta cheese,** crumbled

DRESSING:

½ cup **extra-virgin olive oil**

½ cup **lemon juice**

1 tsp **dried oregano**

1 tsp **salt**

½ tsp **pepper**

In saucepan of boiling salted water, cook barley until tender, about 30 minutes. Drain and rinse under cold water; drain well. Let stand for 10 minutes to dry. Transfer to large bowl.

Meanwhile, in separate saucepan, bring 1½ cups salted water to boil. Add rice; cover, reduce heat and simmer until tender and no liquid remains, about 15 minutes. Let stand for 5 minutes. Add to barley; let cool.

Add tomatoes, onion, red pepper and cucumber to barley mixture; toss to combine.

DRESSING: Whisk together oil, lemon juice, oregano, salt and pepper; pour over salad and toss to coat. Cover and refrigerate for 30 minutes. *(Make-ahead: Refrigerate for up to 24 hours.)*

Just before serving, stir in spinach and feta cheese.

MAKES 12 TO 16 SERVINGS. PER EACH OF 16 SERVINGS: about 194 cal, 5 g pro, 10 g total fat (3 g sat. fat), 22 g carb, 3 g fibre, 12 mg chol, 454 mg sodium, 254 mg potassium. % RDI: 8% calcium, 8% iron, 16% vit A, 38% vit C, 15% folate.

BARLEY

WHY IT'S GOOD FOR YOU: An ancient staple across the globe, barley is high in fibre, including beta-glucan, a soluble fibre also found in oats that helps lower bad cholesterol. Barley also contains manganese, selenium, iron, zinc and some B vitamins. Like wheat, barley contains gluten, so it's off-limits for people with celiac disease or gluten sensitivity.

WHOLE GRAIN FORMS: **Hulled barley** is the kernel of the plant with just the outer hull removed. It contains all of the bran, germ and endosperm. **Pot barley** undergoes a bit of refining, but it is considered a whole grain because a good amount of the bran and germ remains intact. **Whole grain flour** made from hulled barley is available, but check the label to ensure that it is 100 per cent whole grain and not made from refined pearl barley.

STORAGE: Whole grain hulled barley, pot barley and flour contain a lot of healthy natural fat, so they can spoil easily. They will keep for up to a year if sealed in an airtight container in the fridge or freezer.

USES: Barley is versatile, in much the same way as rice. Try it in risottos, soups and stews, or in a delicious grain salad or pilaf. Whole grain barley flour is nice in delicate breads and baked goods because it doesn't have a strong grainy flavour like whole wheat or rye flours do.

From left: Whole grain barley flour and hulled barley

This salad is a symphony of textures: chewy barley, tender-crisp corn and juicy steak. This is a particularly delicious dish to make during the late summer corn harvest, when cobs are at their sweetest.

BEEF, BARLEY & CORN SALAD

2 tbsp **vegetable oil**

1 tsp **chili powder**

½ tsp each **salt** and **pepper**

2 cloves **garlic,** minced

1 lb (450 g) **beef strip loin grilling steak** (1 inch/2.5 cm thick)

4 cups shredded **red leaf lettuce**

SALAD:

2 cups **cooked pot barley**

1½ cups **cooked corn kernels** (about 5 cobs)

1½ cups chopped **tomatoes**

⅓ cup chopped **fresh cilantro**

⅓ cup chopped **red onion**

3 tbsp **extra-virgin olive oil**

3 tbsp **lime juice**

¾ tsp **ground cumin**

¼ tsp **salt**

Stir together oil, chili powder, salt, pepper and garlic; brush over steak. Let stand for 15 minutes.

Place steak on greased grill over medium-high heat; close lid and grill, turning once, until medium-rare, about 8 minutes. Transfer to cutting board and tent with foil; let stand for 5 minutes before thinly slicing across the grain.

SALAD: Meanwhile, in large bowl, combine barley, corn, tomatoes, cilantro, red onion, oil, lime juice, cumin and salt; toss to combine.

Divide lettuce among plates; top with salad. Arrange steak over top.

TIP: To make the amount of cooked barley needed for this recipe, cook ½ cup pot barley in saucepan of boiling salted water, according to package directions for best results.

MAKES 4 SERVINGS. PER SERVING: about 507 cal, 31 g pro, 27 g total fat (6 g sat. fat), 39 g carb, 7 g fibre, 56 mg chol, 760 mg sodium, 781 mg potassium. % RDI: 4% calcium, 32% iron, 36% vit A, 27% vit C, 28% folate.

Cooking tomatoes makes their lycopene easier for the body to use, and creates a tasty dressing for this salad. Enjoy it warm or cold alongside your favourite barbecued main dish.

WHEAT BERRY, BARLEY & TOMATO SALAD

1 cup **hard wheat berries**

1 cup **pot barley** or pearl barley

2 cups **grape tomatoes** or cherry tomatoes

¼ cup **extra-virgin olive oil**

¼ cup **balsamic vinegar**

2 cloves **garlic,** minced

¼ tsp **dried thyme**

¼ tsp each **salt** and **pepper**

¾ cup **goat cheese,** crumbled (about 4 oz/115 g)

2 **green onions,** thinly sliced

Rinse wheat berries; place in bowl. Add enough water to cover by 2 inches (5 cm); let stand at room temperature for 12 hours. Drain.

Bring saucepan of salted water to boil; stir in wheat berries. Reduce heat to medium-low; cover and simmer, stirring occasionally, for 30 minutes.

Stir in barley; cook, covered, until tender, about 30 minutes. Drain well; transfer to large bowl.

Meanwhile, cut tomatoes in half. In skillet, heat oil over medium heat; fry tomatoes, vinegar, garlic, thyme, salt and pepper until warm and softened, about 5 minutes.

Pour dressing over wheat berry mixture; toss to coat well. Stir in goat cheese and green onions.

TIP: To test for doneness of wheat berries, remove a grain and taste; it should be chewy with a soft centre.

MAKES 4 TO 6 SERVINGS. PER EACH OF 6 SERVINGS: about 363 cal, 9 g pro, 14 g total fat (4 g sat. fat), 53 g carb, 7 g fibre, 9 mg chol, 345 mg sodium. % RDI: 5% calcium, 21% iron, 10% vit A, 12% vit C, 15% folate.

A bright Mediterranean-inspired vinaigrette perks up the mild chicken and barley in this main-dish salad. Make a double batch for potlucks or backyard barbecues. To keep it cold, nestle the salad bowl in a larger bowl filled with ice.

GRILLED CHICKEN & POT BARLEY SALAD

2 **boneless skinless chicken breasts**

⅔ cup **pot barley**

1½ cups chopped trimmed **green beans**

1 cup **grape tomatoes,** halved

¼ cup minced **red onion**

2 tbsp chopped **fresh basil**

VINAIGRETTE:

¼ cup **extra-virgin olive oil**

2 tbsp **wine vinegar**

1 tbsp **Dijon mustard**

½ tsp **dried Italian herb seasoning**

¼ tsp each **salt** and **pepper**

VINAIGRETTE: In large bowl, whisk together oil, vinegar, mustard, Italian seasoning, salt and pepper. Transfer 2 tbsp to large shallow dish; add chicken, turning to coat. Cover and refrigerate for 10 minutes. *(Make-ahead: Refrigerate for up to 8 hours.)*

Meanwhile, in saucepan of boiling water, cover and cook barley for 20 minutes. Add green beans; cook until beans are tender-crisp and barley is tender, about 10 minutes. Drain and toss with remaining vinaigrette.

Place chicken on greased grill over medium-high heat; close lid and grill, turning once, until no longer pink inside, about 10 minutes. Cut into cubes.

Add chicken to barley mixture. Add tomatoes, onion and basil; toss to combine.

MAKES 4 SERVINGS. PER SERVING: about 330 cal, 20 g pro, 16 g total fat (2 g sat. fat), 28 g carb, 7 g fibre, 39 mg chol, 653 mg sodium, 497 mg potassium. % RDI: 4% calcium, 15% iron, 13% vit A, 15% vit C, 12% folate.

Beautifully thin and crunchy, this flatbread tastes just as good on the fourth day as the first. You'll find malt syrup in health food stores and some supermarkets.

OATS & WHOLE WHEAT FLATBREAD

1 cup **large-flake rolled oats**

1 cup **whole wheat flour**

¾ tsp **salt**

½ tsp **baking soda**

¼ cup **unsalted butter,** softened

2 tbsp **malt syrup** or buckwheat honey

In food processor, whirl oats until finely ground, about 2 minutes. In large bowl, whisk together oats, whole wheat flour, salt and baking soda. Stir in butter and malt syrup to form soft crumbly dough. With fork, stir in ½ cup water to make soft ragged dough.

With lightly floured hands, press dough into ball; cover and let stand for 10 minutes. Divide in half.

On lightly floured surface, roll out each half into paper-thin 16- x 12-inch (40 x 30 cm) rectangle; prick all over with fork. Transfer to greased or parchment paper–lined baking sheets.

Lightly brush with water; bake in 400°F (200°C) oven, rotating halfway through, until golden and crisp, about 10 minutes. Let cool on pans on racks. Break into pieces. *(Make-ahead: Store in airtight container for up to 1 week.)*

MAKES 2 SHEETS, OR 32 PIECES. PER PIECE: about 38 cal, 1 g pro, 2 g total fat (1 g sat. fat), 5 g carb, 1 g fibre, 4 mg chol, 74 mg sodium, 28 mg potassium. % RDI: 2% iron, 1% vit A, 1% folate.

While not technically made with a whole grain, these muffins contain one of the most nutritious portions of the oat kernel: oat bran. Toasting it brings out its earthy, warm, nutty flavour. The muffin cups will be full, but don't worry; they won't overflow.

BANANA, DATE & OAT BRAN MUFFINS

¾ cup **oat bran**

1¼ cups **all-purpose flour**

2¼ tsp **baking powder**

½ tsp **cinnamon**

¼ tsp each **baking soda** and **salt**

1⅓ cups mashed **bananas**

⅔ cup finely chopped **dates**

½ cup **almond butter** or natural peanut butter

½ cup **milk**

⅓ cup **light-tasting olive oil** or safflower oil

⅓ cup **liquid honey**

1 **egg**

In dry skillet, toast oat bran over medium heat until lightly browned, about 3 minutes. Transfer to bowl; let cool. Whisk in flour, baking powder, cinnamon, baking soda and salt.

In large bowl, stir together bananas, dates, almond butter, milk, oil and honey; stir in egg. Stir in flour mixture just until combined. Spoon into 12 paper-lined or greased muffin cups.

Bake in 375°F (190°C) oven until tops are firm to the touch, about 25 minutes.

Let cool in pan on rack for 2 minutes. Transfer to rack; let cool. (*Make-ahead: Store in airtight container for up to 3 days.*)

CHANGE IT UP
Banana, Fig, & Oat Bran Muffins Substitute finely chopped dried figs for the dates.

MAKES 12 MUFFINS. PER MUFFIN: about 272 cal, 5 g pro, 13 g total fat (2 g sat. fat), 38 g carb, 3 g fibre, 16 mg chol, 143 mg sodium, 308 mg potassium. % RDI: 7% calcium, 12% iron, 1% vit A, 3% vit C, 19% folate.

These wholesome, not-too-sweet muffins are great for breakfast on the go or for a late-morning snack. The recipe also has two fruity variations if you'd like to switch up the flavour.

CARROT, OATMEAL & WHOLE WHEAT MUFFINS

1 cup **quick-cooking rolled oats** (not instant)

¾ cup **whole wheat bread flour**

¾ cup **all-purpose flour**

½ cup packed **brown sugar**

1 tbsp **baking powder**

½ tsp **cinnamon** or ground ginger

¼ tsp **salt**

1 cup **milk**

1 **egg**

¼ cup **vegetable oil**

1 tsp **vanilla**

1 **carrot,** grated

½ cup chopped **walnuts** (optional)

In large bowl, whisk together rolled oats, whole wheat bread flour, all-purpose flour, brown sugar, baking powder, cinnamon and salt.

Whisk together milk, egg, oil and vanilla; pour over dry ingredients. Sprinkle with carrot, and walnuts (if using); stir just until dry ingredients are moistened. Spoon into 12 paper-lined or greased muffin cups.

Bake in 375°F (190°C) oven until cake tester inserted in centre of several comes out clean, about 20 minutes.

Let cool in pan on rack for 5 minutes. Transfer to rack; let cool completely. *(Make-ahead: Store in airtight container for up to 24 hours or wrap individually in plastic wrap and freeze for up to 2 weeks.)*

CHANGE IT UP

Apple, Raisin, Oatmeal & Whole Wheat Muffins

Replace carrot with 1 apple, peeled and grated; replace walnuts with raisins.

Tropical Fruit, Oatmeal & Whole Wheat Muffins

Replace carrot with ¾ cup mixed dried tropical fruit (chopped into ½-inch/1 cm pieces if necessary); replace walnuts with ¼ cup sweetened shredded coconut.

MAKES 12 MUFFINS. PER MUFFIN: about 179 cal, 4 g pro, 6 g total fat (1 g sat. fat), 28 g carb, 2 g fibre, 17 mg chol, 145 mg sodium, 151 mg potassium. % RDI: 7% calcium, 9% iron, 12% vit A, 10% folate.

These muffins are big on flavour and sure to entice even those who have no trouble with gluten. Play around with the fruit: Try dried blueberries, strawberries or raspberries, or chopped dried apricots. Turn to page 13 for information on the special gluten-free baking ingredients you'll need to make this recipe.

GLUTEN-FREE FRUITY OAT MUFFINS

1 cup **wheat-free rolled oats**

⅓ cup **brown rice flour**

⅓ cup **tapioca starch**

⅓ cup **cornstarch**

1 tbsp **baking powder**

1 tsp **baking soda**

¾ tsp **xanthan gum**

½ tsp **cinnamon**

¼ tsp **salt**

½ cup **dried cherries**

½ cup **dried cranberries**

⅓ cup **golden raisins**

½ cup **granulated sugar**

2 tsp each finely grated **orange zest** and **lemon zest**

2 **eggs**

1¼ cups **Balkan-style plain yogurt**

⅓ cup **light-tasting olive oil** or safflower oil

1¼ tsp **vanilla**

1 tsp **cider vinegar**

TOPPING:

⅓ cup **wheat-free rolled oats**

In food processor, pulse oats until almost fine; transfer to bowl. Whisk in brown rice flour, tapioca starch, cornstarch, baking powder, baking soda, xanthan gum, cinnamon and salt; stir in cherries, cranberries and raisins.

In large bowl, rub sugar with orange and lemon zests; whisk in eggs. Whisk in yogurt, oil, vanilla and vinegar. Stir in flour mixture just until combined. Spoon into 12 paper-lined muffin cups.

TOPPING: Sprinkle oats over batter. Bake in 375°F (190°C) oven until tops are firm to the touch, about 25 minutes.

Let cool in pan on rack for 2 minutes. Transfer to rack; let cool. (*Make-ahead: Store in airtight container for up to 2 days.*)

TIP: People with gluten sensitivities or celiac disease should not buy dried fruit or nuts from bulk bins, since the products may be cross-contaminated with gluten-containing ingredients from another bin. (People often use the same scoop in different bins.) It's best to buy sealed containers.

MAKES 12 MUFFINS. PER MUFFIN: about 272 cal, 5 g pro, 10 g total fat (3 g sat. fat), 42 g carb, 2 g fibre, 37 mg chol, 267 mg sodium, 192 mg potassium. % RDI: 10% calcium, 8% iron, 4% vit A, 2% vit C, 4% folate.

These cinnamon-scented delights are less flaky than traditional scones, with more of a muffin texture. If you like raisins or dried cranberries, add ½ cup after cutting in the butter.

OATMEAL SCONES

1¾ cups **all-purpose flour**

1 cup **quick-cooking rolled oats** (not instant)

2 tbsp **granulated sugar**

2½ tsp **baking powder**

½ tsp each **baking soda** and **cinnamon**

¼ tsp **salt**

½ cup cold **butter,** cubed

1 cup **buttermilk**

1 **egg**

TOPPING:
1 tbsp **buttermilk**

1 tbsp **coarse sugar**

In large bowl, whisk together all-purpose flour, oats, sugar, baking powder, baking soda, cinnamon and salt. Using pastry blender or 2 knives, cut in butter until crumbly.

Whisk buttermilk with egg; pour over flour mixture. Stir with fork to make ragged dough.

With lightly floured hands, press dough into ball. On floured surface, knead gently 10 times. Place on parchment paper–lined baking sheet. Pat into ½-inch (1 cm) thick round. Cut into 8 wedges.

TOPPING: Brush dough with buttermilk; sprinkle with sugar. Bake in 400°F (200°C) oven until golden, about 25 minutes.

Let cool on pan on rack for 2 minutes. Transfer to rack; let cool. (*Make-ahead: Store in airtight container for up to 24 hours or wrap in plastic wrap and freeze in airtight container for up to 2 weeks.*)

MAKES 8 SCONES. PER SCONE: about 294 cal, 7 g pro, 14 g total fat (8 g sat. fat), 36 g carb, 2 g fibre, 56 mg chol, 364 mg sodium, 144 mg potassium. % RDI: 10% calcium, 14% iron, 11% vit A, 29% folate.

Whether it's freshly sliced or toasted and spread with butter and jam, this is a fantastic breakfast bread. It's full of flavour and moist yet wonderfully light. It's also a delicious option for your favourite sandwich.

WHOLE WHEAT & OAT SANDWICH LOAF

1 tsp **active dry yeast**

¾ cup warm **water**

2 cups **whole wheat flour**

1 cup **white bread flour** (approx)

⅓ cup **buttermilk** or milk

3 tbsp **liquid honey**

1 **egg,** lightly beaten

1¼ tsp **salt**

¾ cup **large-flake rolled oats**

In bowl, sprinkle yeast over warm water; let stand until granules are swollen, 10 minutes. Stir in ½ cup each of the whole wheat and bread flours. With wooden spoon, beat 100 strokes in same direction until gluey. Scrape down side of bowl. Cover with plastic wrap; let rise in warm place until bubbly and almost tripled in volume, 2½ hours.

Scrape dough into large bowl. Beat in buttermilk, honey, egg and salt until combined. Beat in oats and remaining whole wheat flour. Stir in remaining white bread flour.

On floured surface, knead dough, adding a little more bread flour as needed to make smooth moist dough, for 10 minutes. Place in greased bowl; turn to grease all over. Cover; let rise in warm place until doubled in bulk, 1¾ to 2 hours.

Lightly push down dough. On floured surface, knead lightly; shape into ball, stretching and pinching dough underneath to smooth top. Cover; let rest for 10 minutes.

Flatten into long 1-inch (2.5 cm) thick oval. Starting at long edge, roll into cylinder; pinch seam to seal. Place, seam side down, in oiled 9- x 5-inch (2 L) loaf pan. Cover; let rise in warm place until risen above top of pan, 1 to 1½ hours.

With serrated knife, cut ¼-inch (5 mm) deep slit lengthwise along top. Bake in 425°F (220°C) oven for 15 minutes. Reduce heat to 375°F (190°C); bake until loaf sounds hollow when tapped on bottom and instant-read thermometer inserted in centre registers between 190°F and 200°F (88°C and 93°C), about 25 minutes.

MAKES 1 LOAF, OR 16 SLICES. PER SLICE: about 119 cal, 5 g pro, 1 g total fat (trace sat. fat), 24 g carb, 3 g fibre, 12 mg chol, 189 mg sodium, 105 mg potassium. % RDI: 2% calcium, 9% iron, 1% vit A, 10% folate.

This classic cookie is still a treat, but it comes with the nutritional benefits of whole wheat flour, whole grain oats and dark chocolate. If you prefer, raisins can stand in for the chocolate chips.

WHOLE WHEAT OATMEAL CHOCOLATE CHIP COOKIES

⅔ cup **butter**, softened

1 cup packed **brown sugar**

2 **eggs**

2 tsp **vanilla**

1½ cups **quick-cooking rolled oats** (not instant)

1 cup **whole wheat flour**

½ tsp **baking powder**

½ tsp **baking soda**

¼ tsp **salt**

1 pkg (250 g) **dark chocolate chips**

In large bowl, beat butter with brown sugar until fluffy. Beat in eggs and vanilla.

Whisk together oats, whole wheat flour, baking powder, baking soda and salt; stir into butter mixture. Stir in chocolate chips. Drop by heaping 1 tbsp, about 2 inches (5 cm) apart, onto 2 parchment paper-lined baking sheets.

Bake in top and bottom thirds of 375°F (190°C) oven, switching and rotating pans halfway through, until golden, about 12 minutes.

Let cool on pans on racks for 2 minutes. Transfer to racks; let cool.

MAKES ABOUT 25 COOKIES. PER COOKIE: about 175 cal, 3 g pro, 9 g total fat (5 g sat. fat), 22 g carb, 2 g fibre, 29 mg chol, 101 mg sodium, 132 mg potassium. % RDI: 2% calcium, 11% iron, 5% vit A, 2% folate.

Anzac bickies (short for biscuits) are said to have originated in the trenches of the First World War by or for Australian and New Zealand troops. They have few ingredients, a long shelf life and a healthy dose of whole grain oats.

ANZAC BICKIES

1 cup **all-purpose flour**

1 cup **large-flake rolled oats**

1 cup **unsweetened desiccated coconut**

1 cup packed **brown sugar**

½ cup **butter**

3 tbsp **golden syrup**

In large bowl, whisk together flour, oats, coconut and sugar; set aside.

In saucepan, heat together butter, golden syrup and 2 tbsp water over medium-low heat until butter is melted; stir into dry ingredients. Drop by rounded 1 tbsp, 2 inches (5 cm) apart, onto parchment paper–lined or greased rimless baking sheets.

Bake in 350°F (180°C) oven until light golden on bottoms, about 15 minutes.

Let cool on pans on racks for 2 minutes. Transfer to racks; let cool completely. *(Make-ahead: Store layered between waxed paper in airtight container for up to 1 week.)*

TIP: Golden syrup is a light-coloured liquid sweetener that's also known by the name light treacle. The best-known brand is Lyle's. Look for cans or jars of it in large supermarkets near the honey or corn syrup, or in the baking aisle.

MAKES 24 COOKIES. PER COOKIE: about 129 cal, 1 g pro, 5 g total fat (4 g sat. fat), 19 g carb, 1 g fibre, 12 mg chol, 56 mg sodium. % RDI: 1% calcium, 5% iron, 4% vit A, 4% folate.

Nothing says harvest more than this comforting classic dessert. The whole wheat topping is a little softer than a typical crisp topping, but it has a subtle nutty flavour.

WHOLE GRAIN
PLUM APPLE CRUMBLE

4 cups sliced **plums**

2 cups sliced peeled **apples**

⅓ cup packed **brown sugar**

2 tbsp **all-purpose flour**

¼ tsp **nutmeg**

¼ tsp **cinnamon**

CRUMBLE:

1 cup **large-flake rolled oats**

½ cup **whole wheat flour**

⅓ cup packed **brown sugar**

¼ tsp **cinnamon**

Pinch **salt**

⅓ cup cold **butter,** cubed

Toss together plums, apples, sugar, flour, nutmeg and cinnamon; spread in lightly greased 8-inch (2 L) square baking dish.

CRUMBLE: In bowl, whisk together rolled oats, flour, brown sugar, cinnamon and salt. With fingers or pastry blender, rub or cut in butter until in coarse crumbs. Scatter over fruit mixture.

Bake in 350°F (180°C) oven until bubbly, fruit is tender and topping is golden, 40 to 60 minutes.

MAKES 8 SERVINGS. PER SERVING: about 274 cal, 4 g pro, 9 g total fat (5 g sat. fat), 47 g carb, 4 g fibre, 20 mg chol, 63 mg sodium, 293 mg potassium. % RDI: 3% calcium, 10% iron, 9% vit A, 10% vit C, 5% folate.

Pears add their perfumy aroma to a traditional crisp topped with a crumbly oat mixture. Top it with a spoonful of whipped cream, crème fraîche, frozen yogurt or ice cream.

PEAR APPLE CRISP

6 cups chopped peeled **pears**

2 cups chopped peeled **apples**

2 tbsp **all-purpose flour**

2 tbsp packed **brown sugar**

2 tbsp **lemon juice**

¼ tsp **cinnamon**

TOPPING:

1 cup **quick-cooking rolled oats** (not instant)

½ cup packed **brown sugar**

⅓ cup **all-purpose flour**

Pinch **nutmeg**

⅓ cup **butter,** melted

Toss together pears, apples, flour, brown sugar, lemon juice and cinnamon; spread in 8-inch (2 L) square baking dish. Set aside.

TOPPING: Whisk together oats, sugar, flour and nutmeg. Drizzle butter over top; toss with fork until crumbly. Sprinkle over pear mixture.

Bake in 350°F (180°C) oven until pears are tender and topping is golden and crisp, about 1 hour.

MAKES 6 SERVINGS. PER SERVING: about 430 cal, 5 g pro, 12 g total fat (7 g sat. fat), 82 g carb, 9 g fibre, 27 mg chol, 87 mg sodium, 472 mg potassium. % RDI: 5% calcium, 15% iron, 10% vit A, 20% vit C, 18% folate.

This version of our often-requested recipe uses whole wheat flour instead of all-purpose, boosting the fibre content. The topping is a little soft, so gobble the squares up right away before they get soggy.

WHOLE GRAIN BLUEBERRY OATMEAL SQUARES

2½ cups **large-flake rolled oats**

1¼ cups **whole wheat flour**

1 cup packed **brown sugar**

1 tbsp grated **orange zest**

¼ tsp **salt**

1 cup cold **butter,** cubed

FILLING:

3 cups **fresh blueberries**

½ cup **granulated sugar**

⅓ cup **orange juice**

4 tsp **cornstarch**

FILLING: In saucepan, bring blueberries, sugar and orange juice to boil; reduce heat and simmer until tender, about 10 minutes. Whisk cornstarch with 2 tbsp water; whisk into blueberry mixture and boil, stirring, until thickened, about 1 minute. Place plastic wrap directly on surface; refrigerate until cooled, about 1 hour.

In large bowl, whisk together oats, flour, sugar, orange zest and salt; with pastry blender, cut in butter until in coarse crumbs. Press half into parchment paper–lined 8-inch (2 L) square cake pan; spread blueberry filling over top. Sprinkle with remaining oat mixture, pressing lightly.

Bake in 350°F (180°C) oven until light golden, about 45 minutes. Let cool in pan on rack before cutting into squares.

MAKES 24 SQUARES. PER SQUARE: about 191 cal, 3 g pro, 9 g total fat (5 g sat. fat), 28 g carb, 2 g fibre, 20 mg chol, 84 mg sodium, 115 mg potassium. % RDI: 2% calcium, 6% iron, 7% vit A, 3% vit C, 3% folate.

ACKNOWLEDGMENTS

No matter whose name or face appears on the cover of a book, there are always many other people behind the scenes to thank for their hard work. This book is no exception, and thanks always go first to the excellent staff of The Canadian Living Test Kitchen (whose faces actually *are* on the book!). Without their knowledge and good taste, there would be no Tested-Till-Perfect recipes to share. Special thanks go to Louisa Neumann and Melanie Stuparyk, who created a number of new, delicious and nutrient-packed whole grain recipes especially for this publication.

Two people I am always grateful to in the book-creation process are *Canadian Living* food director Annabelle Waugh and art director Chris Bond. Their sense of humour and drive to create a beautiful, functional book – each and every time – is what makes the job such a pleasure. From selecting recipes to reading the final proofs, they're integral to each step. The new design and fresh approach to healthy eating are the culmination of their collective talents.

Photography is always one of the most exciting parts of creating a publication. I was privileged to watch a very talented team put together a gorgeous new batch of images for this book: photographer Edward Pond, food stylist Nicole Young and prop stylist Madeleine Johari. Their work and the work of many other photographers and stylists (see page 272 for more) was invaluable in making the recipes in this book come alive.

Thanks also go to Austen Gilliland and Janet Rowe for combing through the *Canadian Living* recipe database and helping me assemble the book's lineup. When all the assembling was done, copy editor Jill Buchner went through and dotted all the i's and crossed all the t's (and fixed plenty of stray grammar mistakes).

Beth Zabloski cheerfully took on the task of indexing all the information in this book so that it's organized in easily searchable, logical categories. Sharyn Joliat of Info Access analyzed the nutrient content of each recipe so you can be sure of the nutrition you'll be getting in each dish you make. Random House Canada's team worked together to distribute and promote this book across the country. Thanks to all of them for a job well done.

Support for our cookbooks comes direct from the top of the *Canadian Living* organization. I'd like to thank Transcontinental Books publisher Jean Paré, *Canadian Living* publisher Lynn Chambers and *Canadian Living* editor-in-chief Susan Antonacci for their unwavering confidence in our work, and for challenging us to aim higher with every project.

And to all of our readers, we send out the biggest thank you of all. You make all of this work worthwhile.

– *Christina Anson Mine, project editor*

INDEX

CREDITS

RECIPES

All recipes were developed by The Canadian Living Test Kitchen, except the following.

Louisa Neumann: pages 18, 85, 87, 93, 100, 104, 114, 119, 140, 142 and 146.

Melanie Stuparyk: pages 43, 123, 126, 141, 155, 161, 174, 203 and 206.

PHOTOGRAPHY

Ryan Brook/TC Media: page 5.

Mark Burstyn: page 81.

Jeff Coulson/TC Media: page 117.

Yvonne Duivenvoorden: pages 21, 25, 26, 31, 32, 39, 40, 64, 70, 74, 91, 97, 135, 148, 153, 173, 179, 189, 190, 195, 198, 199, 235, 239, 251 and 260.

Edward Pond: pages 2, 10, 19, 37, 56, 57, 63, 69, 83, 84, 92, 103, 110, 118, 127, 136, 143, 147, 151, 154, 167, 169, 176, 185, 201, 205, 208, 215, 218, 219, 225, 241, 243 and 252.

Jodi Pudge: pages 131, 183 and 259.

David Scott: pages 45, 113, 125, 163, 213, 229 and 244.

Ryan Szulc: page 175.

Andreas Trauttmansdorff: page 53.

Felix Wedgwood: page 129.

FOOD STYLING

Donna Bartolini: page 97.

Lucie Richard: pages 40, 113, 125, 135, 163, 183, 229 and 244.

Claire Stancer: pages 26, 31, 64 and 190.

Claire Stubbs: pages 21, 25, 32, 53, 70, 131, 148, 153, 189, 195, 198, 199, 251 and 260.

Rosemarie Superville: pages 45, 81 and 173.

Nicole Young: pages 2, 10, 39, 56, 57, 63, 69, 74, 84, 91, 92, 103, 117, 118, 127, 129, 136, 147, 154, 167, 179, 201, 205, 208, 213, 218, 219, 225, 235, 239, 243, 252 and 259.

PROP STYLING

Laura Branson: pages 148 and 229.

Catherine Doherty: pages 25, 39, 53, 70, 74, 81, 91, 117, 131, 173, 179, 183, 195, 198, 199, 235, 239 and 251.

Madeleine Johari: pages 2, 10, 19, 32, 37, 56, 57, 63, 69, 83, 84, 92, 103, 110, 118, 127, 136, 143, 147, 151, 154, 167, 169, 176, 185, 189, 201, 205, 208, 215, 218, 219, 225, 241, 243 and 252.

Oksana Slavutych: pages 21, 26, 31, 40, 45, 64, 97, 113, 125, 135, 153, 163, 190, 213, 244, 259 and 260.

Genevieve Wiseman: page 129.

ILLUSTRATION

Courtesy of **Oldways and the Whole Grains Council** (wholegrainscouncil.org): page 11.